About the Author

Noel Whelan MA is a history and politics graduate of University College, Dublin and was called to the Bar in 1998. He is a practising barrister on the Dublin and South Eastern Circuits and has written on politics and elections. He is the co-author of *Malinhead to Mizenhead – The Definitive Guide to Local Government in Ireland* (1992) and *The Tallyman's Guide to the 1999 European and Local Elections* (1999).

He has also worked as a political organiser at Fianna Fáil national headquarters and was a candidate in both the 1997 Dail and Seanad Elections.

Politics, Elections and the Law

Noel Whelan

Barrister-at-Law

BLACKHALL
Publishing

This book was typeset by Artwerk for

Blackhall Publishing
8 Priory Hall
Stillorgan
Co. Dublin

e-mail: blackhall@eircom.net
www: blackhallpublishing.com

© Noel Whelan, 2000

ISBN: 1 901657 69 8 pbk

A catalogue record for this book is available from the British Library.

Printed in Ireland by
ColourBooks

Contents

PREFACE

On a summer's afternoon in 1997 I had reason to do a number of library searches on the topic of electoral law. To my surprise there was an almost complete absence of texts, articles, or directories of caselaw in this area.

The combination of political science and legal studies, which has been my own academic path, prompted me to redress this deficit by putting together the first Irish text dedicated to this area of law. It turned out to be a more challenging task then I had realised.

This book is the result of those efforts. It aims to meet the needs of both political and legal practitioners. It should sit as well on the shelf of public representatives, local government officials, journalists or political commentators as it should on that of any solicitor or barrister who may find themselves dealing with queries or cases relating to the workings or activities of the political world.

I hope that I have charted a careful course between the need to be comprehensive and the need to create a reference book, which is accessible in both language and format to a wider audience. Where it might have been cumbersome to include particular material the reader has been referred to further reading or information by way of footnote.

This work is based largely on the original statutes covering electoral law in Ireland. The growing body of legislation in the area of ethics and campaign funding is also covered. It would have been too cumbersome to incorporate the many statutes relevant to the area as part of this publication. In any case, in this age of statutes on CD-Rom and Internet search engines it would probably also have proved unnecessary.

The emphasis has been on summarising or explaining the statutory provisions rather than repeating them in the various chapters. The one exception is in the chapter on Miscellaneous Campaign Law where for ease of reference the sections of the various statutes are repeated. The constitutional provisions relevant to the areas covered by the book are also included in a separate section again for ease of reference.

This desire for an easy flowing text has also prompted me to put the case law into a separate section at the back. I have sought to include much of the case law relevant to the areas covered. The objective in the case notes has been to give a snap shot of the judgements and in particular the elements which are most relevant to electoral and campaign law and to the law as it currently stands. Where the cases have been more extensively reported elsewhere I have included the references.

There are many legal topics that touch on elections and politics, which fall outside the remit of this current work. For example there is a large range of legislation and information relating to parliamentary procedure, as well as payments and allowances to politicians which might have been incorporated. These gaps together with forthcoming legislative initiative and evolving judicial activity in this area already point to further editions of this or a similar work. Some of the areas, which have attracted proposals for reform, are analysed in the final chapter.

In order to minimise the use of the somewhat clumsy phrases 'he or she' and 'him or her' the masculine possessive pronoun is used predominately throughout this book. This reflects the unfortunate reality that males dominate in almost all the positions and offices with which we are dealing. In recognition of the unique exception of the office of the presidency, at least in recent years, the feminine version is used in chapter nine. Where the Minister is used, unless other wise specified, it can be taken to refer to the Minister for the Environment and Local Government, more usually described as the Minister for the Environment.

All errors and omissions remain the author's responsibility alone, and I would be grateful to be notified of any such. To the greatest extent possible this work states the law as of May 2000.

I am grateful to many people for their assistance in researching and writing this book. Many have read individual chapters, provided insights or sourced elusive material. In particular I would like to thank the Franchise Section of the Department of the Environment and Local Government, Brian Allen and the staff of the Public Office Commission and Deirdre Lane Clerk of the Seanad. I am grateful to all the staff at the Law Library issue desk for their patience and assistance. I owe a special thanks to my former colleague at Fianna Fail HQ, Sean Sherwin whose knowledge of the intricacies and practicalities of the operation of Irish elections has few equals. Thanks also to Hugh Dolan and Vincent Hoy for particular insights.

I am grateful also to many colleagues at the Law Library who offered or were prevailed upon for assistance. A particular word of thanks goes to Colm O'hOisin BL, Richard Humphreys BL and Brian Lenihan SC, who undertook the review of, and added much to, the final manuscript. On a general level I owe a particular thanks to Deirdre Murphy SC, who taught me so much about the law and more importantly about the purposes to which the law should be put.

I wish to thank those who made it possible at Blackhall Publishing and in particular Gerard O'Connor.

Jim Mitchell T.D. has done us the great favour of writing the forward for this book and has added his own pertinent perspective on the law in these areas.

The final word of thanks must go to Sinead McSweeney who not only applied much of her proof reading, sub-editing and political skills to earlier drafts but also put up with my time being diverted to this and other projects, especially over the summer months.

Noel Whelan
Four Courts, Dublin
May 2000

FOREWORD

Interest in politics wafts and wanes. It all depends on the intensity of current issues and chemistry of, and between, current political leaders. The interest in political and electoral mechanisms however, is ever present and comes to a height as an election approaches.

Yet, the knowledge of electoral law is very poor even among political activists. This book will help to fill that void because of its comprehensive citation of the many Acts which impinge on elections and politics.

The book is being published amidst pressing calls from Noel Dempsey, Minister for the Environment and Local Government for change in our system of proportional representation. It also comes in the wake of the strong recommendations from the Committee of Public Accounts in its D.I.R.T. Report for fundamental reform and modernisation of the Oireachtas.

I have long espoused the view that our present electoral system has several serious flaws. Most notably, because coalition and/or minority governments have been with us almost continuously since 1973. The danger of the Government falling suddenly is a constant concern. As a result there is an aversion to taking long-term decisions necessary in any society but which might be temporarily unpopular or which, at least, might not yield any immediate political benefit.

These concerns are heightened if by-elections are pending or if Presidential, local or European elections are due.

For the above reasons among others I have long favoured two basic changes viz.:

1. Dáil casual vacancies to be filled by co-option rather than by-election. This only requires a change in the law. This is already the position regarding vacancies in local authorities and the European Parliament.

2. A fixed term Dáil. This change certainly would require a Constitutional Amendment. It is already the position in local authorities and the European Parliament and in several National Parliaments in the E.U., and in the U.S.

These changes would also help to make the life of TDs a little easier and would allow for better planning by them and by Government and by political parties. The present uncertainty is a disincentive to successful people seeking election to the Dáil. More importantly it hampers consistent and advance planning by the State.

These changes have no implication for the electoral system but I have also long believed that some changes are required to the present electoral system (provided that any new system is still proportional) so as to focus deputies more on national affairs and less on constituency affairs.

Variations of the German proportional representation system are often mooted and are worth considering.

Remember the German P.R. system was introduced following the disaster of the Weimar Republic in which an ever splintered Reichstag made government impossible over a prolonged period and which led directly to the ascent of Hitler to power.

Its main features are:

1. 50 per cent of Bundestag seats are filled in one seat constituencies on the first past the post system;

2. However, a party or group which falls below 5 per cent of the national vote must win a minimum of 3 constituencies to hold any constituency;

3. To get a share of the 50 per cent of seats on the list a party must win a minimum of 5 per cent of the national vote;

4. Votes of all parties or groups with less than 5 per cent are discounted and the percentage of parties over 5 per cent is re-totalled. The new percentage is then applied to the total number of seats in the Bundestag. From this number the total of constituencies won is subtracted and the remainder is the number of list seats to which the party is entitled;

5. The lists are drawn up in each Lander (State) rather than nationally.

If we were to adopt the German system with some Irish variations we should not reduce its 5 per cent threshold of the national vote. Suggestions that the threshold be reduced to 2 per cent are dangerous and have Weimar Republic-like potential. However, this threshold could be one of two parallel but alternative thresholds the other being say 10 per cent of the vote in any Euro-constituency and/or province. In other words if a party got 5 per cent or more of the national vote or 10 per cent or more of the vote in any Euro constituency then all its votes nationally would count and they would get the appropriate percentage of Dáil seats.

Another obvious variation would be to use the single transferable vote in filling the one seat in each constituency and the winner is the winner in each constituency with no minimum three-seats rule.

A third variation would be to vary the mix between constituencies and the list from the German 50/50 to say 66 per cent constituencies and 33 per cent list.

And finally, constituencies might be two-seaters rather than single seaters. Two seaters would ensure Government and opposition representation in every constituency and yet reduce the present level of repetition of representations from 3, 4 or 5 TD's and several more prospective TD's. It would also eliminate the destructive in fighting within Parties in multi-seat constituencies, which is such a feature of the present Irish P.R. system.

A list system also offers the opportunity, if we are motivated to do so, to provide for a certain proportion of gender balance as in the Nordic countries.

However, the selection and prioritisation of the list, whether it be national or regional, is a major issue which, if established wrongly, could give party headquarters too much influence. This is already a deadening factor in all parties in Ireland.

Regardless of the electoral system, a fixed term parliament gives better scope for ensuring that the electoral register is up to date. It would also make the granting of votes easier to Irish citizens temporarily abroad – an issue on which Ireland is way behind many other States. Moreover, in a fixed term scenario the option of making voting compulsory, as in Australia, becomes more feasible.

Finally, recent legislation imposing funding limits and declaration on ethics has imposed new constraints on parties and candidates. Some of the requirements are ludicrous and impose unrealistic demands. Worse still they have shifted the balance further in the direction of centralised control in each party, which, in my opinion, is already, an unhealthy and dangerous feature of Irish politics.

Moreover, the small minority of candidates who have no scruples will have no difficulty in making false declarations as to spending thus putting the larger majority who are honest at a disadvantage. We can hardly introduce lie detector tests to overcome this problem.

Of more immediate importance is the urgent need for the modernisation of the Dáil itself. Some fundamental changes have been proposed in the PAC Report on D.I.R.T. But they are only headlines.

The Oireachtas has 3 basic functions:

1. To elect or fire a government

2. To hold government to account

3. To enact legislation.

Many more changes are needed if the Oireachtas is to undertake, more conscientiously, parts 2 and 3 of its remit. Those changes are within the compass of the Dáil itself and are crying out to be implemented.

Politics has been made a great deal more complex by the many changes to the law introduced in recent years. This book will be of considerable assistance to all those involved or interested in the political or electoral process. It will prove to be an indispensable reference book.

Jim Mitchell T.D.
Chairman,
Committee of Public Accounts

Table of Cases

Table of Statutes

Table of Statutory Instruments

Table of Statutory Instruments

Table of Constitutional Provisions

1 Constituencies and Electoral Boundaries

History of constituency revisions

Article 16.2 of the Constitution[1] provides that the Dáil is to be composed of members "who represent constituencies determined by law". Originally, the practice had been for the government to revise the constituencies and present that revision to the Dáil as it would any other bill. This procedure invariably gave rise – on occasion with some justification – to opposition allegations of gerrymandering.

Since 1970, ad hoc commissions have been established to advise and report on the revision of constituencies. In recent times, the government has implemented the reports presented by these commissions without amendment.

This procedure for the revision of constituencies and the drawing of constituency boundaries by an independent committee was put on a statutory footing by Part II of the Electoral Act 1997. This Act provides for an independent constituency commission to come into being each time the constituencies are to be revised.

Timing of constituency revisions

The Constitution requires that Dáil constituencies must be revised at least once in every twelve years. However, the Constitution also requires that there be equality of representation, so far as is practicable, throughout the country. In practice, this means that the Constitution requires a revision of constituencies after each population census, especially when there are any significant geographic shifts in population.[2]

Hamilton P put it succinctly in *O'Malley v An Taoiseach*[3]

> The constitutional obligation placed on the Oireachtas is not discharged by revising the constituencies once in every twelve years. They are obliged to revise the constituencies with due regard to changes in distribution of the population

---

1. See page 181.
2. See Part II of the Electoral Act 1997, section 5 to 15.
3. See page 168.

and when a census return discloses major shift in the distribution of the population there is a constitutional obligation on
the Oireachtas to review the constituencies.

The Electoral Act 1997 now lays out a procedure for the revision of constituencies, which automatically occurs once a population census has been
completed.[4] Although population censuses are usually carried out once
every five years, this is not necessarily always the case, and so the constituency revisions may occur at longer intervals.

Statutory Constituencies Commission

Establishment
The 1997 Act provides that, on publication by the Central Statistics Office
of a census report, following each census of the population, the Minister
for the Environment must establish a constituency commission to review
both Dáil and European constituencies.

It is important to note that a constituency commission is not established
as a permanent entity. A constituency commission comes into existence
only for the duration of its work and dissolves once its report has been
delivered to the Ceann Comhairle, which must be within six months.

Membership
The 1997 Act also lays down rules governing membership of the constituency commission. The commission is chaired by a judge of the
Supreme Court or High Court, nominated by the Chief Justice. There are
four other members: the Ombudsman, the Secretary of the Department of
the Environment, the Clerk of the Dáil and the Clerk of the Seanad.[5] The
commission is serviced by staff assigned by the Minister for the
Environment.

Independence
The members are required to act independently in their role as members of
the commission. The Electoral Act 1992 makes it an offence, punishable
by a fine of up to £1,000, to attempt to communicate (apart obviously from
submissions) with the staff of the commission or a member of the commission for the purpose of influencing the commission in carrying out its
functions. The members and staff of the commission are also required to

---

4.   See Part II of the Electoral Act 1997, section 5 to 15.
5.   There is provision for the deputies of these officeholders – except the judge obvious-
     ly – to serve on the constituencies commission when the respective office is vacant
     or the officeholder is incapacitated.

maintain confidentiality about its work, a breach of which is also punishable by a fine of £1,000.

Report
The commission must seek public submissions, usually by advertising in the national press. The commission is required to deliver two reports – one on Dáil constituencies and another on European constituencies to the Ceann Comhairle of the Dáil. This must be done as soon as possible and, as stated above, not later than six months after its establishment.

Criteria for constituency revisions
The basic parameters within which constituencies and electoral boundaries can be shaped are set down by the Constitution. These are elaborated on in the Electoral Act 1997. This Act sets out the criteria to which the constituency commission must have regard. It also details the terms of reference for the revision of Dáil and European constituencies, subject to the overriding constitutional requirements.

Number of representatives per constituency
Although the Constitution does not specify the exact membership of the Dáil, it does provide that there must be no less than one member of the Dáil per 30,000 people and not more than one per 20,000 of the population.[6] It is worth reiterating that this ratio is seats to population of all ages and not seats to number of electors.

The Constitution also provides that each Dáil constituency must return a minimum of three deputies. Legislation lays down that the maximum number of deputies per constituency is five.[7]

For a number of years after independence, some constituencies returned up to nine members, but, since 1954, no constituency has had more than five members.

Proportional representation
The Constitution also requires that there be equality of representation so far "as is practicable" throughout the country.

In *O'Donovan v Attorney General*[8] the scheme of revision of constituencies in 1959 was struck down as unconstitutional because it infringed the requirement for equality of ratio and representation. Budd J. held that

---

6. Article 16.2.2°, see page 181.
7. Section 6, Electoral Act 1997.
8. See page 162 and [1961] IR 114.

"as far as practicable" it implied the need to have regard to difficulties of an administrative or statistical nature. He rejected the suggestion that factors, such as geographical difficulties, sparsely populated areas, travelling and greater demands on deputies' time were relevant and would justify greater representation for western constituencies.

The new revision of constituencies necessitated by this judgment was framed in the Electoral (Amendment) Act 1961. In light of the *O'Donovan* case, the President referred the 1961 Act to the Supreme Court.[9]

In its judgment, the Supreme Court said:

> exact parity in the ratio between members and the population of each constituency is unlikely to be obtained and is not required. The decision as to what is practicable is within the jurisdiction the Oireachtas...It is a decision not to be reviewed by the courts unless there is a manifest infringement of the Article. This court cannot as is suggested, lay down a figure above or below which a variation from what is called the national average is not permitted. This is of course not to say that a court...may not pronounce on whether there has been such a serious divergence from the uniformity as to violate the requirements of the Constitution.

Similarly, the relevant legislation provides that when the commission is defining the boundaries of European constituencies, it is required to achieve reasonable equality of representation as between them.

Contiguous areas

The Electoral Act 1997 requires that the constituency commission, in considering both Dáil and European constituencies, must seek to ensure that each constituency be composed of contiguous areas, that the breaching of county boundaries shall be avoided as far as practicable and that there be regard to geographic considerations, including significant physical features and the extent of and density of population in each constituency.[10]

Subject to these considerations, the commission is also required to maintain continuity in relation to the arrangement of constituencies.

Of course, it is open to the commission, having reviewed the constituencies under the above criteria, to recommend that there be no revisions. This was the conclusion of the 1998 Constituency Commission's report on European constituencies.

---

9.   *In the Matter of the Electoral Amendment Act 1961.* See page 160 – and [1961] IR 169.
10. See section 6, Electoral Act 1997.

Local authorities and local electoral areas

Provisions relating to the revision of local authority areas and to the number and boundaries of electoral areas within a local authority are laid out in the Local Elections Act 1991.

The local authority area is the functional area in which a local authority operates. An electoral area is effectively a local constituency for the local authority, i.e. the area from which a designated number of members is to be elected. Unlike the situation, which pertains to Dáil Éireann, there are no express constitutional restrictions on the number of council members of any local authority or the number of electors that each council member should represent.

Electoral areas
The subdivision of a local authority's functional areas into electoral areas, if any, is determined by ministerial order. In general, smaller local authorities are not subdivided and the full membership of the council is elected to represent the entire council area.

Boundary committees
The law provides that the Minister for the Environment can establish one or more boundary committees to advise him in respect of the revision of local authority areas or local electoral areas. The committee can have three to five members, who are all appointed by the minister, and the minister also appoints one of them to be chairperson. A TD, Senator, MEP or member of a local authority cannot be appointed to a boundary committee. A local authority official can be a member of a boundary committee, however, he cannot be involved in a decision relating to his own local authority or any authority within that functional area.

The 1991 Act specifies that a boundary committee shall be independent in the exercise of its functions, that it can seek public submissions and hold oral hearings and that it must consult with any local authority likely to be affected by its recommendations.

Terms of reference of boundary committees
Although the Act does not set down criteria to which boundary committees must have regard, it does state that the Minister may provide the committees with terms of reference.

In 1997, the Minister appointed two boundary committees – one to make recommendations on the subdivision of the four Dublin local authorities into electoral areas, and one to make recommendation on the division into local electoral areas of local authorities outside Dublin. The committees reported in July 1998, and their recommendations for the revision of areas were implemented in full by ministerial regulations the following October.[11]

The terms of reference given to the two committees required them to advise on the division of the local authority into electoral areas and the number of members of the council to be assigned to each with a view to ensuring a reasonable relationship between the 1996 population and the representation within each local electoral area. The committee was asked in their review to have regard to:

- the objective of drawing up a local electoral areas, which (alone or in combination) would as far as practicable have an urban or neighbourhood focal point and would be of such size as would facilitate the decentralisation of local authority and other services;

- the desirability of preserving natural communities or areas forming the hinterland of population centres (or shopping centres in Dublin);

- outside Dublin, the desirability where it may be possible to do so of aligning county electoral area boundaries with Dáil constituency boundaries;

- a requirement that the number of councillors representing an area in a county or county borough should be not less than three but not more than seven.

---

11. See Electoral Area Boundary Committee Report 1998.

2 Franchise and the Register of Electors

Right to vote in different polls

Only a person whose name is included on the register of electors can vote in an election or referendum.[1]

Apart from age and citizenship requirements and the need to be on the electoral register, there are no bars to the right to vote. There are no constitutional or statutory prohibitions to voting by prisoners or the insane. This means, for example, that an elector currently serving a prison sentence, if on day or temporary release, could cast his vote at the polling station for which he is registered.

Previously, persons convicted of corrupt or illegal practices or of an electoral offence were disqualified from voting, but this disqualification was repealed by the Electoral Act 1963.

The elections in which an individual is entitled to vote are determined by citizenship and residency.

- Irish citizens whose names are included on the register of electors are entitled to vote in referenda, presidential elections, European elections, Dáil elections and local elections.

- British subjects may vote in Dáil elections, European elections and local elections. This entitlement derives from the reciprocal right of Irish citizens resident in Britain to vote in similar elections.

- Nationals of other European Union (EU) Member States may vote in European and local elections, but they may vote in Dáil elections only when reciprocal arrangements exist for Irish nationals resident in the particular Member State.[2]

- Non-EU citizens may vote only in local elections.

---

1. The law relating to the registration of electors is set out in Part II of the Electoral Act 1992 and the Second Schedule to that Act. See also section 76 of the Electoral Act 1997 in reference to the supplementary register.
2. At present, no such reciprocal arrangements exist.

The extension of the voting right in Dáil elections to British citizens and potentially nationals of other European Member States was brought about by the passing of the Ninth Amendment to the Constitution by referendum in 1985. The right to vote in Dáil elections can be extended by ministerial order – where the Minister is satisfied that the laws of an EU Member State allow an Irish citizen resident in that State to vote in elections to its national parliament, reciprocal arrangements can be made for citizens of that Member State to vote in Dáil elections.

Age requirement

Every resident aged 18 years and upwards on the day the register comes into force (15 February) is entitled to be on the register and vote. If one becomes 18 during the life of a register, one is entitled to be entered on the supplementary register, details of which are outlined below. The previous age requirement of 21 was reduced to 18 by the Fourth Amendment to the Constitution, which was passed by referendum in 1972.[3]

Residence requirements

A person must be ordinarily resident in a registration area on the qualifying date – currently the first day of September in the year preceding the coming into force of the register. Similarly, if one establishes residence during the life of a register, one is entitled to be entered on the supplementary register.

If a person has more than one address (e.g. a person living away from home to attend college or in connection with employment), the registration authority should be told for which address the person wishes to be registered.

Section 11(3) of the Electoral Act 1992 provides that a person who leaves his/her ordinary residence with the intention of returning there within eighteen months can continue to be registered there, subject to the overriding condition that a person may be registered at one address only. A written statement by the person that they intend to return within eighteen months in the absence of evidence to the contrary is accepted as correct.

A person who is absent on a temporary basis from his/her ordinary address – for example, on holiday, in hospital or abroad in the course of employment – should be registered for that address. A visitor or person staying temporarily at the address should not be registered for that address.

A person who on the qualifying date is a patient or inmate in a hospital, home or mental hospital can be registered at their home address, or if that cannot be ascertained at the address where they last resided.

---

3.   The 9th Amendment to the Constitution see Article 16.1.2° at page 181.

A member of the permanent defences force resident in a barracks can, if he so chooses in writing, be registered at the address at which, but for his service, he would be ordinarily resident.

An Irish civil servant serving abroad and his spouse living abroad are deemed to be ordinarily resident on the qualifying date at the address in Ireland, which, but for the requirement of his duty, they would be resident.

Prohibition on double registering

Although the Constitution expressly provides at Article 16.1.4° that a person can only vote once in an election, it does not prohibit double registration per se. In *Quinn v City of Waterford*,[4] a group of students of what was then Waterford Regional Technical College argued that they were ordinarily registered in Waterford during the academic year and at their home constituencies out of term. McCarthy J., for the court, agreed with them and held that Article 16.1.4° prohibits double voting, not double registration. The Supreme Court upheld the students' claim and rejected an argument that, in order to avoid double voting, it was necessary to prohibit the registration of voters in more than one constituency.

However, section 11 of the Electoral Act 1992 now specifies that a person shall not be registered as an elector more than once in any registration area or in more than one registration area.

Preparation of the register of electors

The registration authority (the relevant county council or corporation) in each registration area is required by law to prepare and publish a register of electors every year.[5] The register comes into force on 15 February and is used at each election or referendum held in the following twelve months.

In practice, the council or corporation begins the process of preparing a register by making house-to-house enquiries or other local enquiries in September and October. This task is delegated to the relevant urban council or corporation in urban areas within a county council. In many instances, this will involve delivering registration (RFA) forms to households for completion. The registration campaign is usually reinforced by an advertising campaign by the Department of the Environment in national press and broadcast media.

A draft register is then published on 1 November and made available for inspection in post offices, Garda stations, public libraries and other public buildings. Members of the public are invited to check the draft register to make sure they are correctly registered. Claims for corrections to the draft registration must be made before 25 November each year.

4.   See page 171 and [1990] 2 IR 507.
5.   Section 20, Electoral Act 1992.

Claims to amend the draft register are adjudicated on by the county registrar. The registrar's rulings are made in public and any person may attend and give evidence. The registrar must, unless he is satisfied the person is dead, give at least five days notice to the claimant and to the person in respect of whom the claim is made of the time and place at which the claims will be considered. The county registrar's decision can be appealed to the Circuit Court.

Supplementary register

Section 15 of the Electoral Act 1992 empowers registration authorities to prepare and publish a supplementary register. The public is notified of this facility when an election or referendum is called so that those who are not on the current register of electors can arrange to be included on the supplementary register.

The 1992 Act provides that a person who, on the qualifying date, was entitled to be but was not actually on the register, may apply to the registration authority to have his name entered on the register of electors.[6] Section 76 of the Electoral Act 1997 went even further by providing that a person, who was not resident in the constituency on the qualifying date for the main register of electors but who has since taken up ordinary residence in the constituency and is otherwise entitled to be registered, can apply and be registered on the supplementary register. In a similar manner, any person, who is otherwise entitled to be registered, who was not 18 years on the qualifying date for the ordinary register but has since reached the age of 18 can now apply and be registered on the supplementary register.[7]

Application for entry on the supplementary register must be received by the registration authority at least fifteen working days before polling day in order to be considered for that election or referendum.

This supplementary register is deemed to form part of the register of electors. Each registering local authority must publish a copy of the supplementary register for its area.

Persons entered in the supplementary register are entitled to vote at all appropriate polls held during the currency of the register, i.e. until the new register takes effect the following February, by which time they will be included on the main register.

Postal voters list

Each registration authority prepares a postal voters list as part of the register of electors. Applications for inclusion in the postal voters list must be

---

6. Section 15, Electoral Act 1992.
7. Section 76, Electoral Act 1997.

received by 25 November at the latest. An elector registered as a postal voter may vote by post only and may not vote at a polling station.

A number of categories of persons may be registered as postal voters.

- Whole-time members of the defence forces can be postal voters. Members who live in military barracks may be registered either at the barracks or at their 'home' address.

- Irish civil servants serving abroad and their spouses also have postal votes and are registered at the addresses they would be ordinarily resident in Ireland were they not required to be at their foreign posting. They must send a statement to the registration authority in their 'home' constituency indicating where they propose to register and enclosing the required certification from the Department of Foreign Affairs.

- Members of the Garda Síochána have the option of being registered as ordinary electors or as postal voters. In either case, they are registered at their home address.

Section 63 of the Electoral Act 1997 gave the right to another category of electors to be registered on the postal voters list:

- persons whose occupation, service or employment means that they are unlikely to be able to go to their local polling station on election day.

The 1997 Act defines occupation, in this instance, to include participation on a full-time basis on an educational course in an educational institution in the State. Consequently, students who are likely to be away from their ordinary residence (at which they are registered) during term time can apply for a postal vote in their 'home' constituency. The registration authority may require additional information or documents from an applicant in this category seeking to be included on the postal voters list. If such information or documentation is not furnished within a reasonable period, the application is deemed to have been withdrawn.

In this instance, the application to go on the postal voters list must be made before 25 November and must be accompanied by a certificate from the employer in the case of an employed person and, in any other case, by a statutory declaration.

The procedure for voters included on the postal voter list by virtue of section 63 of the 1997 Act is different from that for diplomats, gardaí and members of the defence forces, in that the elector must bring the ballot paper and declaration of identity which they receive in the post to a garda station where the declaration identity must be witnessed by a garda and stamped with the station stamp.[8] In the case of diplomats, gardaí and members of the defence force there is no requirement to attend at a garda station, the elector merely completes the declaration of identity himself or herself and returns it with the ballot paper to the returning officer.[9]

A supplementary postal voters list is also prepared, although it is not open to members of the defence forces or diplomats posted abroad. The latest date for receipt of supplementary applications for the postal voters list is the date of dissolution of the Dáil in the case of a general election and the date of the order appointing polling day in the case of Dáil by-elections, a presidential election, a European election, a local election or a referendum.

Special voters list
As part of the register of electors, registration authorities also prepare a list of special voters composed of electors with a physical illness or disability living in hospitals, nursing homes, etc. who wish to vote at these locations. In order to qualify, an elector's physical illness or disability must be likely to continue for the duration of the register and prevent him from going to a polling station to vote.[10]

Applications to be entered on the special voter list must be made by 25 November and, in the case of a first application, must be accompanied by a medical certificate.

Electors on the special voters list vote at their hospital, nursing home, etc. by marking a ballot paper delivered to them by a special presiding officer accompanied by a garda.

A supplementary special register is also prepared.

Dates and deadlines
The various dates and deadlines in the procedure for compelling the register are specified in the second schedule of the 1992 Act as follows:

*   *Qualifying date (for age and residence determination)*
    1 September in the year proceeding the year in which the register comes into force;

8. Sections 63 to 65, Electoral Act 1997.
9. Electoral Act 1992.
10. Section 17, Electoral Act 1992.

- *Period for giving notice in relation to special voting*
  Period of fourteen days ending on 1 September;

- *Last date for sending of statement to registration authority by civil servants serving abroad*
  25 November;

- *Last date for receipt of application to be entered on the special voters list*
  25 November;

- *Publication of draft register*
  1 November;

- *Last date for making claim for addition or deletion form the register*
  25 November;

- Publication of list of claims for addition/deletion from register
  30 November;

- *Publication of register of electors*
  1 February;

- *Coming into force of register*
  Fourteen days after publication of the register;

- *Period for ascertaining if any corrections in the register are necessary because of errors of a clerical or typographical nature or because of misnomers or inaccurate descriptions*
  Fourteen days commencing on the date of the publication of the register.

Entitlement to copies of the register of electors

The registration authority is required to send a copy of the draft register in November and a copy of the finalised register in February to:

(a) for a registration area (i.e. a county or borough corporation) to the minister, the county registrar, and each head postmaster in the area;

(b) for a European parliament constituency, to each MEP for that constituency;

   (c) for a Dáil constituency, to each member of Dáil Éireann for that
      constituency and to each member of Seanad Éireann residing in the
      constituency;

   (d) for a local electoral area, to each local authority member for that
      area.

Each candidate's election agent in any election is entitled to one copy of
the electoral register free of charge for the relevant constituency or electoral area.

3 Voting Procedures

Format of the ballot paper

The format of the ballot paper in each election is specified in the relevant legislation.[1] Generally, the ballot paper must contain the names and descriptions of the candidates as set out on the nomination paper. The Acts also provide that the names must be arranged alphabetically in order of surname. When surnames are the same, they will be arranged in the alphabetical order of first name. If two or more candidates happen to have the same first and surname, the returning officer must draw lots to determine the order in which they should appear on the ballot paper.

In *O'Reilly v Minister for the Environment*,[2] the constitutionality of the alphabetical arrangement of the names on the ballot paper was challenged. Upholding the requirement, Murphy J. in the High Court commented that the alphabetical listing of candidates on the ballot paper "poses the practical advantage – particularly in a constituency where a number of candidates present themselves – that the voter can quickly find any particular candidate".

The legislation is very specific as to the format and layout of ballot papers and even goes so far as to detail the typeface in which the candidates' names should appear. The candidate's surname and party affiliation or the designation "NON PARTY" must be in capital letters. The first name is to be printed in small capitals and the address and occupation, if any, as appearing on their nomination paper is printed in "ordinary characters", i.e. lower case. The space on the ballot paper given to the name, address and description of each candidate must be the same.

The Act also provides that a ballot paper shall be numbered consecutively on the back and that the back of the counterfoil attached to each ballot paper shall bear the same number.

Marking the ballot paper[3]

The voter indicates the order of his choice by writing the number 1

---

1. Section 88, Electoral Act 1992.
2. See page 169.
3. Section 17, Electoral Act 1992.

opposite the name of his first choice and, if he so wishes, the number 2 after his second choice, the number 3 opposite the name of his third choice, and so on. In this way, the voter instructs the returning officer that, when the vote is counted, his vote should be transferred to the second choice candidate if the first choice candidate is either elected or eliminated. If the voter's second choice has also been elected or eliminated, the vote may be transferred to the third choice, and so on.

The secrecy of the ballot

The Constitution provides that Dáil and presidential elections and referenda must be conducted by secret ballot. There is a legislative provision for a similar secrecy requirement in European elections. The courts have taken a strict view of this constitutional requirement.

In *McMahon v Attorney General,*[4] the Supreme Court struck down as unconstitutional the practice of writing a voter's register of electors number on the counterfoil of ballot papers. The basis for the decision was that, when this number was coupled with the numbering of the ballot paper and its counterfoil, there arose a possibility, however slight, that a voter's ballot paper could be identified. In the High Court, Pringle J. held that "the words 'secret ballot' in Article 16.4[5] mean a ballot in which there is complete and inviolable secrecy".

The various electoral acts reinforce the requirement that the casting of a vote should be kept absolutely secret in a number of ways:

- The returning officer must provide polling booths – "compartments in which the voter can mark their ballot papers screened from observation".[6]

- There is a general legal requirement imposed by the 1992 Act on any person present at the issue of postal ballot papers, present while special voters are voting, present at the opening of postal ballot boxes or admitted to a polling station in any capacity at a polling station or at the counting of votes to maintain and aid in maintaining the secrecy of the ballot.

- Any person who is present in any capacity at the counting of votes at an election is guilty of an offence if, except for some purpose authorised by law, he ascertains or attempts to ascertain at such

---

4. See page 167.
5. See Article 16.1.4°.
6. See *Dillon-Leetch v Calleary*, page 156.

counting the number on the back of a ballot paper or, if at any time, he communicates any information obtained at such count as to the candidate for whom any vote is given on any ballot paper.

- The Electoral Act 1992 requires that, at the count, the ballot papers, when being counted, are faced upward in order to keep the ballot paper number on the back from view.

- The Electoral Act 1992 also protects the secrecy of the ballot against enquiry by any court – "a person who has voted at a Dáil election shall not in any legal proceedings be required to state for whom he voted".[7]

Procedure for voting at a polling station

- The elector applies in person at the polling station, to which he is assigned, for a ballot paper giving his name and address.

- The number on the register and name of the elector as stated on the register is called out. A person's name is taken to be on the register if there is a name on the register, which, in the opinion of the presiding officer, was intended to be the person's name. Therefore, a man who is generally known as Seamus Smith may have been registered as James Smith and, provided that there was no other James Smith on that street, the presiding officer is likely to hold that name to be the same person.

- The ballot paper is then marked with the official mark.

- The elector's name on the register is marked to show that a ballot paper has been issued in respect of the elector. The mark must in no way indicate the number of the ballot paper issued.

- The voter then goes alone to the polling booth to mark the ballot paper, folds the ballot paper and returns to the presiding officer's table to drop it into a ballot box.

Proof of identity and prevention of personation

Personation is the offence of applying for a ballot paper in the name of some other person, whether that other person is dead or alive, or applying

---

7. See, for example, section 162 of the Electoral Act 1992 as it pertains to Dáil elections.

for a ballot paper in one's own name where one has already obtained a ballot paper at the same election.

There are three steps which a presiding office may take if he has concerns as to a voter's identity, age or whether the voter has already cast a vote in that election.

Proof of identity

A presiding officer on his own motion may, and, if asked by any candidate's personation agent in the polling station, must, request any person to produce proof of identity. The proof of identity must be sought before the ballot paper is issued and cannot be sought after the ballot paper is issued. The electoral acts and regulations provide that a range of specified documents can serve as proof of identity. This list of documents is printed on the polling card sent to all electors. Acceptable proofs of identity include an employment identity card, a social welfare book or ID card, a passport or a driving licence.

If a person who is requested to produce proof of identity fails to do so, or if the presiding officer is not satisfied that the person is the person to whom the document relates, then that individual is not permitted to vote.

Questions to an elector

The presiding officer may on his own motion, and, if asked by any candidate's election agent present at the polling station, must, put a set of specified questions to any person:

- Are you the same person as the person whose name appears as AB on the register of Dáil electors now in force for the constituency of X?

- Have you already voted in this election X?

- Had you reached the age of 18 on (date of coming into force of the register/supplementary register)?

Unless the person answers yes to the first question, no to the second and yes to the third question, that person is not allowed to vote.

Oath/Affirmation

The presiding officer on his own motion may, and, if asked by a personation agent for any candidate, must, administer the following oath to any person:

> I swear by almighty God (or do solemnly, sincerely and truly declare and affirm) that I am the same person as the person

whose name appears as AB on the register of Dáil electors now in force for the constituency of XX and that I have not already voted at this election and that I had attained the age of eighteen years on YY (the date of coming into effect of the register).

The oath can be made as an affirmation by any person who objects to taking an oath on religious grounds, or who has no religious belief.

If, when a person presents to the polling station for a ballot paper, it emerges that a ballot has already been given to another person in respect of that name on the register, the second person can still be issued with a ballot paper, after providing proof of identity and taking the required oath/affirmation. The presiding officer returns to the returning officer with the ballot box a note to the effect that he has issued a second ballot paper for that name.

Procedure for postal voting

Candidates are entitled to nominate agents to be present at the issuing of postal ballot papers. Each postal ballot paper must be embossed with the official mark.

The procedure for voting by persons who are on the postal voters' list because they are civil servants posted abroad, gardaí or members of the defence forces is relatively straightforward.

As soon as practicable after the close of nominations the returning officer posts to each such elector, a ballot paper together with a declaration of identity, a ballot envelope and a cover envelope. The completed ballot paper is placed in a sealed envelope and that sealed envelope and the declaration of identity duly signed are then placed into a covering envelope and must be returned by post to the returning officer before the close of poll.

The procedure for voting by persons in the postal voters list under the Electoral Act 1997 is laid down in section 58 of that Act.[8] A ballot paper is again posted to the elector's registered address. The elector then takes the ballot paper to any garda station. Having produced satisfactory evidence of identity and completed a declaration of identity, which is witnessed and stamped by a garda, the elector will mark the ballot paper in secret in the garda station and subsequently send it with the declaration of identity by post to the returning officer.

Procedure for voting by special voters

Special voters vote at their home or other place of their choosing. A special

---

8. See Chapter 2 on Franchise and Register of Electors.

presiding officer, accompanied by a garda, attends at the special voter's home (or other location) and presents the special elector with a declaration of identity, which the elector signs and the special presiding officer witnesses. The special returning officer then embosses a ballot paper with the official mark and presents it together with the ballot paper envelope to the special elector.

No person other than the special presiding officer, the garda and the special elector should be present when the special elector is voting. The special elector marks the ballot paper in secret, folds it and places it in the ballot paper envelope, which is sealed and placed together with the declaration of identity into a covering envelope. A label signed by both the special presiding officer and the garda is attached to the covering envelope. The special presiding officer is then responsible for ensuring that the envelope is delivered to the returning officer before the close of poll.

Arrangements for voting by electors with a disability

An elector with a physical disability can apply to the returning officer to vote at an alternative polling station if their local station is inaccessible. There is also provision for assistance in voting at the polling station by a companion or the presiding officer where a person is visually impaired or has a physical disability, which would cause them difficulty in voting. Where a person is assisted by a companion, the companion must be over 16 years of age, must not have connection to any candidate and can assist only a maximum of two voters in any one poll.

The presiding officer may also assist persons with reading difficulties who cannot vote without help. One of the arguments advanced for the extension of the use of candidate photographs on ballot papers to Dáil, local and presidential elections is that it too would assist voters with reading difficulties.

Proposals for electronic voting

Interestingly, the Local Elections (Disclosure of Donations and Expenditure) Act 1999 made provision for research – using the counted ballot papers from the 1999 European and local elections – into the feasibility of introducing electronic methods of recording and counting votes under the present PR-STV election system.[9] During the course of the bill's passage through the House, the Minister for the Environment stated that, depending on the results of this research, the government would explore the possibility of introducing electronic voting at some stage for future elections. Electronic voting systems have also been "field tested" during recent by-elections.

---

9. Section 25, Local Elections (Disclosure of Donations and Expenditure) Act 1999.

4 Organisation of the Poll

This chapter aims to outline the detailed arrangements for the organisation of the poll in Dáil, Seanad, European, presidential and local elections and referenda. The arrangements are in the main laid down in the Electoral Act 1992 and, save where otherwise stated, can be taken to apply to all elections. In any case, this chapter should be read in conjunction with the specific chapter that deals with each poll.

Register of political parties

The 1992 Act details the provisions for the maintenance of a register of political parties.[1] The Act specifies that the Clerk of the Dáil shall be the registrar of political parties for this purpose. A party can apply to be registered as a party organised in the State or in part of the State for the purpose of contesting a Dáil election, European election or local election. The Clerk is obliged to register any party that applies, which, in his opinion, is a genuine political party and is organised in the State or part of it to contest a Dáil, European or local election.[2]

The registration form must include the name of the party, the address of party headquarters and the names of the officers of the party authorised to sign certificates authenticating the candidature of candidates at elections.

If the party satisfies the Clerk that a member of the party who is an MEP is a member of a political group formed in accordance with the rules of the European Parliament, then the name of that European parliamentary group is noted with the party's registration. In this way, the name of the European parliamentary group to which a candidate belongs can be included with the name of the Irish political party he represents on the ballot paper for European elections.

The Clerk can refuse to register a party name, which is unduly long, or, in his opinion, resembles the name of a party already on the register such as to be calculated to mislead or confuse the voter.

Although it is necessary for a political party only to apply once to be registered, the Clerk must write annually to each party asking them if they

---

1. See Part III of the Electoral Act 1992.
2. See *Loftus v Attorney General,* page 163 and [1979] IR 221.

wish to remain on the register, and if they do not reply in the affirmative within 21 days he may delete that partly from the register.

The registrar's ruling on any application for entry in the Register of Political Parties must be published in *Iris Oifigiúil*.

The registrar's decision can be appealed to a special Appeal Board, which is composed of a High Court judge, the Ceann Comhairle and the Cathaoirleach of the Seanad.

The party affiliation of candidates appears under the candidate's name on ballot papers in Dáil, European and local elections but no party affiliation appears on the ballot paper in presidential or Seanad elections.

Appointment of returning officers

The officeholder who is to act as returning officer in each constituency for Dáil elections is laid down by law. Where a constituency is wholly within one county or county borough, the returning officer is the county registrar. In the case of Cork city (Cork County Borough), Dublin city (Dublin County Borough) and Fingal, South Dublin and Dun Laoire-Rathdown the returning officer is the City or County Sheriff. Where a constituency incorporates or straddles more than one county or county borough, the Minister for the Environment appoints the register (or sheriff) for one of those counties to be the returning officer for that constituency. In this instance, the returning officer who is appointed can appoint the register of the other county or counties to be assistant returning officers in respect of that part of the constituency which is in their county.[3]

Where there are a number of constituencies within one county or county borough, the registrar can appoint deputy returning officers to conduct the count, and, if the registrar wishes, to accept nominations for some of those constituencies.

By way of illustration, in the 1997 general election, the Wexford County Registrar was automatically the returning officer for the Wexford constituency, the Kilkenny County Registrar was appointed as the returning officer for the Carlow-Kilkenny constituency with the Carlow County Registrar assisting, and, in Dublin City, the City Sheriff was the returning officer for the five constituencies within the Dublin County Borough and appointed deputy returning officers to conduct the count in four of those constituencies.

In European elections, the returning officer is appointed by the Minister for the Environment from among the Dáil returning officers within that Euro-constituency. The Minister for the Environment also appoints the returning officer for presidential elections or referenda, who is usually an

---

3. See Part V of the Electoral Act 1992.

official in the Department of the Environment.[4] In each of these instances, the Dáil returning officer for each constituency assists as the local returning officer in the conduct of European, presidential or referendum polls.

Polling scheme and polling places

At least once every ten years, each county council or county borough council, in consultation with the Dáil returning officer, makes a scheme dividing the county or county borough into polling districts for Dáil, European or local elections and appoints a polling place for each polling district. The polling place must be such as to give electors in that polling district reasonable access to it, even though technically it need not be in the polling district, or even the county or county borough. The polling scheme for each county or county borough must be approved by the Department of the Environment.

Legislation gives the returning office the right to use schools (primary or secondary) and local authority premises as polling stations free of charge.[5] Where the schools are adjacent to or form part of a religious or church complex the school's manager can lodge an objection to their use with the returning officer.

Polling stations

There is a distinction between polling places and polling stations. Technically the polling place is the building complex where voting is held, and, as is outlined above, the polling scheme must designate a polling place for each polling district. A polling place may contain a number of polling stations. When electors enter the polling place, they may be assigned by street or number to different points at which they get their ballot paper. It may be possible to visualise the school or hall as being the polling place and each set of tables where the ballot papers are issued as a polling station. The local returning officer must also make arrangements to provide the equipment, furniture, ballot boxes, copies of the register, pens, stationery and other items required for the poll.

Date and opening hours of poll

The polling day for all elections and for referenda is set by an Order of the Minister for the Environment. The Minister also orders the opening time for polling stations, which must be at least twelve hours, and those twelve

---

4. Peter Greene, Principal Officer, Franchise Section, Department of Environment was returning officer for the 1997 Presidential Election and the 1998 and 1999 referenda.
5. See section 93, Electoral Act 1992.

hours must be between 8 am and 10.30 pm. The poll must be held on the same day in all polling stations and constituencies.[6]

An exception is allowed in the case of polling on offshore islands.[7] A returning officer can make special arrangements to have polling on an island held on an earlier date. This provision is to ensure that the ballot boxes can be transported to the count in time to be counted with the rest of the votes for that constituency.[8] However, polling must not be held earlier than six days before the polling day on the mainland.

Notice of poll
The returning officer must publish a notice of poll, which is usually displayed at post offices, libraries, Garda stations and other public buildings and in local newspapers. This notice of poll must include the date on which the poll will be held, the hours during which the poll will be taken, the names and descriptions of the nominated candidates, the name of their proposers, if any, and the order in which the names will appear on the ballot paper.

Polling cards
The returning officer must issue a polling 'information' card to each elector whose name appears on the main register of electors and who has a vote in that election.[9] Polling cards are not sent to postal voters or electors on the special voters' list. For local elections, local authorities have a discretion not to issue polling cards. The polling card that is posted to each ordinary elector must include details of the voter's number on the register, the polling station at which he will be entitled to vote, and details of the forms of identification which can be used as proof of identity if required. It is important to note that the receipt of a polling card is not a prerequisite to voting. Any elector, eligible to vote in that election, who appears on the register and who produces sufficient proof of identification, if required, is entitled to vote even if they have not received a polling card.[10]

Official mark
Importantly, the Act also provides that when a ballot paper is being issued,

---

6. See section 96, Electoral Act 1992 for provision regarding Dáil elections.
7. See section 85, Electoral Act 1992.
8. Notwithstanding this provision, the declaration of the Galway West result (and the national result) in the 1997 presidential election was delayed for several hours by a delay, due to bad weather, in getting some of the Aran island ballot boxes to the count centre.
9. See section 92, Electoral Act 1992.
10. For a judicial view on the purpose of polling cards, see *Dillon Leetch v Calleary* page 156.

it must be marked with 'an official mark', a special authenticating mark achieved by causing the ballot paper to be either embossed or perforated so as to be visible on both sides of the paper.[11]

The significance of the requirement for 'an official mark' on each ballot paper is underlined by the fact that any ballot paper that does not contain such a mark is deemed to be a spoilt vote, which cannot be included in the count. Many of the hours, in many of the re-counts held in recent Irish elections have been spent in the detailed scrutinising of individual ballot papers to ascertain whether they are marked with this official mark. Where more than one poll is held on the same day the same official mark must be used for all polls.

Presiding officers

The returning officer appoints a presiding officer at each polling station.[12] The presiding officer has overall responsibility for the conduct of the poll at each polling station. The presiding officer is assisted by polling clerks and assistant polling clerks at each station. Polling staff who are electors in that constituency and who will not be able to get to their own polling station can be permitted to vote instead in the polling station where they are working. The presiding officer has an important range of powers including the power to request the arrest of a person in certain circumstances.[13]

Election agents

In Dáil elections, a candidate may appoint one election agent to assist him generally in relation to the election.[14] The candidate or the election agent can attend themselves or appoint others to attend at the issue of ballot papers to postal voters, at the opening of the postal ballot boxes and at the counting of votes. The returning officer can fix the maximum number of such agents that each candidate can appoint in order to ensure that the same number shall be allowed on behalf of every candidate.

Personation agents

Each candidate, or the election agent on the candidate's behalf, can appoint one person to be a personation agent at each polling station to assist the presiding officer in preventing personation.[15]

---

11. See section 89, Electoral Act 1992.
12. See section 95, Electoral Act 1992.
13. See Chapter 11 on Election Offences Penalties and Powers of Arrest.
14. See section 59, Electoral Act 1992.
15. See section 164, Electoral Act 1992.

The opening of the polling station

Immediately prior to the opening of the poll, the presiding officer must show each ballot box to those at the polling station to show that it was empty at the start of the poll.

Prohibition on campaigning at polling stations

Section 147 of the Electoral Act 1992 introduced a prohibition on canvassing, the display of election posters or the use of public address systems for campaigning within 50 metres of the entrance to any polling station on polling day. The prohibition operates from 30 minutes before the opening of the poll to 30 minutes after the close of the polling station.[16] To breach this prohibition amounts to an offence punishable on summary conviction by a fine of up to £1,000 and/or imprisonment for up to six months and, on conviction on indictment, to a fine of up to £2,500 and/or to imprisonment for up to two years.

Section 106 of the Act also requires the presiding officer at each polling station to ensure as far as practicable that all campaign material is removed from the polling station and its grounds.

The closing of the polling station

There is provision for the returning officer to refuse entry to any voter into the polling place once the closing time has passed, however the presiding officer can continue to allow any electors on the premises at that time of closing to proceed to vote. The presiding office must then seal each ballot box, attach the key of each box and then seal in separate packets, all unused ballot papers, the marked copies of the register, the counterfoils of the ballot papers, a ballot paper account, and marking instruments, unused stationery and other documents and materials relating to the election.

Control of access and maintenance of order at polling stations

The Act gives the presiding officer the specific power to ask a member of the Garda Síochána to remove any person from the polling station who misconducts himself or fails to obey the lawful orders of the presiding officer. There are also powers given to the presiding officer to require a garda (or for the garda on his own motion) to arrest somebody on suspicion of personation.[17]

---

16. See also page 78.
17. See Chapter 11 generally.

Special arrangements when two polls are held on the same day

Where any two or more of a Dáil election, European election, presidential election, local election, Údarás na Gaeltachta election or referendum poll are being held on the same day then the law provides that the following must happen:

- The polls must be taken at the same time, in the same place and in the same manner.

- The same official mark must be used for the ballot papers for each poll.

- The ballot papers at each poll must be a different colour.

- The same ballot boxes can be used or different ballot boxes can be used for each poll. If different ballot boxes are used a ballot paper can not be rejected just because it is put in the wrong ballot box.

- An authorisation by a returning officer for an elector to vote in one of the polls at a polling station other than his own polling station extends to all the polls.

- If one person is a candidate in more than one poll he has still the right to free postage in respect of each poll but he may send a combined postal communication, which includes material in relation to both polls.

In addition, the Minister for the Environment may make orders to facilitate or expedite the completion of the polls together and the counting of the votes. Such directions can include the doubling up of different returning officer and presiding officer functions and the issuing of combined polling cards for all the polls.

The 1997 Act provides for the change of a presidential election date that has already been set by ministerial order, where the Dáil is dissolved before the original presidential election day and it is desired to have both the presidential election and Dáil election on the same date.

Special arrangements when the poll is obstructed

The legislation provides for a number of scenarios where polling is obstructed or cannot be completed. A presiding officer can request a garda to remove any person who misconducts himself at a polling station or fails to obey the orders of the presiding officers. There is also provision, where the poll at any polling station is obstructed by violence, for the poll to be adjourned until the following day. The same opening hours must apply to the adjourned poll.

Where for any reason, including damage to a polling station, polling is obstructed, the poll at that station can be suspended. In such a circumstance, the returning officer and the Minister must be informed and, if necessary, the polling at that station can be held on a later date within the next seven days. In a scenario where any ballot boxes or ballot papers are unlawfully taken out of the custody of the returning officer or presiding officer or are tampered or defaced in any way, then the poll at every polling station at which any of those ballot papers or ballot boxes were used is declared void, and the Minister must then take whatever steps he thinks proper for the taking of a fresh poll.[18]

Emergency or special difficulty

Where it appears to the Minister for Environment that there is an emergency or special difficulty the Minister can by ministerial regulation or order, amend or modify any statutory provision relating to the registration of electors, the conduct of an election or referendum.[19]

However, notwithstanding the emergency or special difficulty the order or regulation must comply with the principles laid down in the relevant acts as a whole and every order made under this provision must be laid before each house of the Oireachtas as soon as possible after it is made and can be annulled by a resolution of either house within 21 days.

---

18 For a judicial consideration of when and how the minister should use this power, see
    Sherwin v Minister for the Environment page 172.
19. Section 165, Electoral Act 1992.

5 Dáil Elections

Composition of the Dáil

Article 16 of the Constitution provides that the number of members of the Dáil cannot be more than one for every 20,000 of the population or less than one for every 30,000. Within this limit the ratio of population to members must be the same "so far as is practicable". There are currently 166 members of the Dáil, which represents approximately one member of the Dáil for every 21,000 people. With the exception of the outgoing Ceann Comhairle, all of these members are directly elected to represent specific constituencies.

Duration of a Dáil

The Constitution provides that the same Dáil shall not continue for a period longer than seven years. It also provides that a shorter period can be fixed by law. Since 1927, the law has provided for a maximum period of five years and this limit is currently laid down in section 33 of the Electoral Act 1992. There is no minimum period for the duration of a Dáil.

Of course, the Dáil term does not coincide with the life of a government. The whole government is deemed to have resigned when a Taoiseach resigns. A change of leadership of the governing party therefore can terminate the life of a government without ending the Dáil term. There can also be a change of governing party without an election, even though some 60 years passed before such a change of government without an election occurred.[1]

Dissolution of a Dáil

The President, on the advice of the Taoiseach, may dissolve the Dáil at any time. Where a Taoiseach retains the majority support of the Dáil, the President must assent to his request for dissolution. However, Article 13.2.1° of the Constitution provides that where a Taoiseach has failed to retain the support of a majority in the Dáil, the President may, in her

---

1. A Fine Gael/Labour/DL government led by John Bruton replaced an Albert Reynolds led Fianna Fáil/Labour government in December 1994 without an ensuing general election.

absolute discretion, refuse to dissolve the Dáil. This provision has not been invoked by any president to date.

The Constitution requires that the proclamation issued by the president bringing about dissolution must set out the date of the dissolution of the outgoing Dáil and the date on which the new Dáil will meet. Article 16.4.2° provides that the election of members to the new Dáil must take place not later than 30 days after the dissolution. The electoral acts limit this further by requiring that the election take place between the 17th and 25th day (excluding Sundays and public holidays) after the dissolution of the outgoing Dáil.

Upon the issue of the presidential proclamation dissolving the Dáil, the Clerk of the Dáil must issue a writ to the returning officer in each constituency directing him to cause an election to be held of the full complement of Dáil members who serve that constituency. The date of the poll is designated by order of the Minister for the Environment.

Re-election of the Ceann Comhairle

The Constitution requires that the member of the Dáil who holds the position of Ceann Comhairle immediately before the Dáil is dissolved is, if he so desires, automatically deemed to be elected to the new Dáil. The detailed mechanism for this automatic re-election is laid down in legislation.[2] In normal circumstances, the outgoing Ceann Comhairle is deemed to be re-elected for the constituency for which he was elected in the outgoing Dáil. That constituency will then elect one member less than its allotted number of seats in the election for the incoming Dáil. It follows therefore that if the outgoing Ceann Comhairle was elected for a three-seat constituency, that constituency would be effectively a two-seat constituency for the purpose of the new election.

Returning officers and the notice of election

The Electoral Act 1992 stipulates who will act as returning officer for each Dáil constituency. In each case it is the county registrar, or county sheriff, of the county or county borough, part or all of which is covered by the constituency.[3] Within two days of receiving the writ, the returning officer must publish a notice of election giving the time and place at which nomination papers can be obtained, the time and place where he will receive nominations, the closing date for nominations and the time and date of polling.

2.   Section 36, Electoral Act 1992.
3.   See Chapter 4 on Organisation of the Poll.

Eligibility for membership of the Dáil

Every citizen of Ireland who is over 21 years of age on polling day and who is not disqualified by the Constitution or by law is eligible to be a member of the Dáil. In 1972, a constitutional referendum reduced the voting age for the Dáil from 21 to 18 years. However, the age limit for Dáil membership was not reduced.

The citizenship requirement means that even though citizens of the United Kingdom or other European Union Member States may be entitled to vote in Dáil elections, they are not entitled to stand for election unless they are also an Irish citizen. It should be noted that whereas one is required to be on the register of electors in order to vote in a Dáil election, a candidate is not required to be on the register of electors in the specific constituency, or in any constituency, in order to stand for election.[4]

Incompatible offices

The Constitution itself renders the holding of certain offices incompatible with election to the Dáil. The President cannot be a member of the Dáil or the Seanad and an individual cannot be a member of both Houses of the Oireachtas simultaneously. Article 33.3[5] prohibits the Comptroller and Auditor General from being a member of either House, and Article 35.3[6] imposes the same prohibition on any member of the judiciary. Contrary to some misconceptions, the Attorney General can be a member of either House, and, on three occasions, a member of the Dáil has simultaneously served as Attorney General.[7]

Ineligibility

Section 41 of the Electoral Act 1992 deems the following categories of people ineligible for membership of the Dáil:

A person who:

- is not a citizen of Ireland,

- has not reached the age of 21 years,

- is a member of the Commission of the European Communities or is

---

4. For example, Austin Currie TD was not on the electoral register in Dublin West when first elected a TD for that constituency or on the register for any constituency in the Republic.
5. See page 186.
6. See page 186.
7. For example, John Kelly TD was Attorney General in 1981.

a judge, advocate general or registrar of the Court of Justice of the European Community;

- is a member of the Court of Auditors of the European Community;

- is a member of the Garda Síochána;

- is a full-time member of the Defence Forces;

- is a civil servant who is not by the terms of his employment expressly permitted to be a member of the Dáil;

- is a person of unsound mind;

- is undergoing a sentence of imprisonment for any term exceeding six months, whether with or without hard labour, or of penal servitude for any period imposed by a court of competent jurisdiction in the State; or

- is an undischarged bankrupt under an adjudication by a court of competent jurisdiction in the State.

Where a person elected to the Dáil is appointed to any of the offices mentioned, or becomes ineligible under one of the above incapacities, he ceases to be a member of the Dáil. In most cases, this loss of membership is immediate. In the case of bankruptcy, a sitting member of the Dáil is given a six month reprieve to have the bankruptcy annulled or discharged before being required to give up his seat. In the case of a criminal conviction, the loss of membership does not become effective until after an appeal or the deadline for an appeal has passed. Members of the Oireachtas are not permitted to serve on the boards of most State boards and semi-State companies.

Membership of the European parliament is not yet legally incompatible with membership of the Dáil or Seanad even though some political parties have adopted a policy of prohibiting members from holding seats in both the Oireachtas and the European parliament. In some instances, this involves opting for one or other parliament at the general election following election to the European parliament.

Similarly, ordinary members of the Dáil and the Seanad are not prohibited from being members of local authorities. Ministers, Ministers of State and the Chair of either House are so prohibited. There are proposals to prohibit all Oireachtas members from serving on local authorities at some stage in the future.[8]

Eligibility to vote

Every citizen of Ireland and the United Kingdom and of some other European Union Member States who is on the register of electors is entitled to vote in Dáil elections provided they have reached the age of 18 years on the day the register came into force.[9]

Nomination of candidates

The nomination of candidates in each constituency is overseen by the returning officer for that constituency. A candidate may nominate him/herself or be nominated with his consent by another person who is registered as a Dáil elector for that constituency.[10]

The returning officer must rule on the validity of a nomination within one hour of its presentation. The returning officer is required to object to the name of the candidate if it is not the name by which the candidate is commonly known, if it is misleading and is likely to cause confusion, is unnecessarily long or contains a political reference.

The returning officer is also required to object to the description of a candidate, which is, in his opinion, incorrect, insufficient to identify the candidate or unnecessarily long. The candidate or the returning officer may amend the particulars shown on the nomination paper. The returning officer may rule a nomination paper invalid only if it is not properly made out or signed.

A candidate can withdraw his nomination at any time up to 12 noon on the last day for the receipt of nominations. A withdrawal must be notified in writing to the returning officer.

Deposit by candidates

Section 47 of the Electoral Act 1992 requires that a candidate at a Dáil election, or someone acting on his behalf, must deposit £300 with the returning officer before the close of nominations. It further provides that if a candidate fails to do so he will be deemed to have withdrawn his candidature.[11]

---

8. This proposal is contained in the Local Government Bill, 2000.
9. See also Chapter 2 on Registration of Electors and Franchise.
10. See Part X, Electoral Act 1992.
11. For a consideration of the constitutionality of this deposit requirement see *Redmond v Minister for the Environment, page 177.*

The deposit is returned if:

- the candidate withdraws his candidature;

- his candidature is declared invalid;

- he dies before the polls close;

- he is elected; or

- he is not elected but the greatest number of votes credited to him at any stage of the count is greater than one quarter of the quota.

If a candidate stands in more than one constituency, irrespective of his showing, he will only be returned the deposit made on his behalf in one constituency.

Party affiliation

The Electoral Act provides for the maintenance of a formal register of political parties by the Clerk of the Dáil.[12] A candidate may include on his nomination paper the name of the registered political party he represents. In these circumstances, the nomination paper must be accompanied by a certificate of political affiliation, signed by the authorised officer of the political party in accordance with the provisions for the registration of political parties. The party affiliation will then appear in capital letters under the candidate's name on the ballot paper.

Where a candidate does not represent a registered party he can choose to be described as 'Non Party' on the ballot paper or leave the appropriate space blank.

Arrangements following the death of a candidate

Arrangements following the death of a candidate vary depending on the stage in the nomination and election process at which the death occurs.

If the candidate dies at least 48 hours before the close of nominations, his candidature is deemed to have been withdrawn. If the candidate dies any time after 48 hours before the close of nominations but before the opening of the poll, then the procedure up to that point is cancelled, nominations are reopened and a new nomination date and a new polling date, if required, are set for that constituency. It is not necessary for any of the candidates already nominated before the death to be renominated.

---

12. See 'Register of Political Parties', Chapter 4 on Organisation of the Poll.

If a candidate dies during polling hours all votes are disregarded and all ballot papers destroyed. The nomination and election procedures are started afresh in that constituency and a new polling date is set for that constituency by the Minister for the Environment. Where a candidate dies after the polls close, then the count proceeds in the usual manner. If the deceased candidate is deemed elected that seat is automatically deemed vacant and a by-election is held in the usual manner.

If the outgoing Ceann Comhairle dies after the dissolution of the Dáil but before a writ has been issued in respect of his constituency, then the election proceeds in the usual manner in that constituency to elect the full number of members. If the Ceann Comhairle dies after a writ is issued but before the close of poll in his constituency then the election process is started afresh in the same way as if a candidate had died. Again nominations are reopened and a new polling date for that constituency is fixed. It is not necessary for any of the candidates already nominated before the death to be renominated.

The poll and count
The returning officer in each Dáil constituency is responsible for the conduct of the poll, the detailed arrangements for which are outlined in separate chapters.[13]

Declaration of the result
Having completed the count, the returning officer for each constituency endorses on the writ the names of the person elected for that constituency and forwards it to the Clerk of the Dáil. Each elected member is notified by the Clerk to attend and sign the roll of members. At the first meeting of the Dáil after the general election and before any other business is conducted, the Clerk makes a report about the issue of writs for the election and announces to the House the names of the Members returned to serve for all constituencies.

Dáil by-elections
The Constitution leaves it to be determined by law how casual vacancies in Dáil membership are to be filled. This procedure is laid down in the Electoral Act 1992 and in Dáil Standing Orders. After the vacancy arises, the Dáil passes a resolution directing the Ceann Comhairle to direct the Clerk to issue a writ to the returning officer for the holding of an election

---

13. See especially Chapter 4 on Organisation of the Poll, and Chapter 3 on Voting Procedure.

to fill the vacancy. No time limits are set down for the passing of the resolution.

There is no legal requirement that a vacancy is filled at all, and, where a vacancy has arisen a short time before a general election, the seat has been left vacant until the ensuing general election. It is likely, however, that where a seat was left vacant for an excessive period, it could be challenged on the grounds of the constitutional requirement of proportionate representation.[14]

Tradition dictates that where the vacancy has occurred owing to the death of a member, the writ will not be moved until at least a month has passed since the death. The tradition also has been that it is for the former member's own political party to move the writ. Consequently, the manner in which the vacancy arose, the timing of any other election or referendum with which the by-election could be held simultaneously, the length of term the current Dáil has left remaining and, more pertinently, the balance of voting strength between the parties will all influence the timing of the holding of a by-election.

The procedure for the nomination of candidates, the arrangement of the poll and the conduct of the count in Dáil by-elections are the same as in a general election with the obvious exception that the whole constituency is effectively a one-seat constituency for the purposes of the count. Obviously, if two vacancies emerge in the same constituency at the same time or in close proximity to each other, they can both be filled at the same by-election and the constituency will be treated as a two-seater for the purpose of the count. It is worth noting that, where the Dáil constituencies have been revised since the last election, even where the revising legislation has been passed, any by-election will be conducted on the basis of the constituency boundary in place at the time of the preceding general election. Moreover, a person who is currently a member of the Dáil cannot be a candidate in a Dáil by-election.[15]

---

14. See Chapter 1 on Constituencies and Electoral Boundaries.
15. Not to be confused with a member who resigns his seat and then seeks re-election in the by-election created by his own resignation.

6 The Electoral System and the Counting of Votes

Proportional representation with single transferable vote

The Constitution provides that elections to the Dáil and Seanad and to the office of president must be by proportional representation with single transferable vote (PR-STV). Legislation has provided that the same PR-STV electoral system is to be used for European and local elections. There have been two attempts to amend the Constitution by referendum to change the PR-STV electoral system for Dáil elections. Both of the proposed constitutional amendments were rejected.[1] It is worth noting that a referendum would not be required to change the voting system for local or European elections. The enactment of reforming legislation would be sufficient as it is a legislative rather than constitutional requirement.

A consideration of the merits or demerits of PR-STV, and whether it achieves the objective of being truly proportionate or whether it gives rise to inefficiency and duplication in representation is beyond the scope of this book, which is a work of electoral law rather than a political science treatise. For our purposes, it is necessary to examine the law governing the operation of the system, how ballot papers are marked and how votes are counted in accordance with this electoral system.[2]

Multi-seat constituencies

The PR-STV electoral system is complicated, particularly since it operates in Ireland on the basis of multi-seat constituencies, i.e. where more than one member is elected for each constituency.

For the purposes of Dáil elections, the country is currently divided into 41 constituencies with representation ranging from a minimum of three seats to a maximum of five seats.[3] For European elections, the country is

---

1. Notwithstanding this, see a consideration on a current proposal to change the electoral system in Chapter 20.
2. See generally Part XVIII and Part XIX of the Electoral Act 1992 for the arrangements and rules for the counting of votes.
3. The Electoral (Amendment) Act 1999 provides that for the election of the 29th Dáil, the country will be divided into 42 constituencies.

divided into four constituencies – Dublin, Leinster and Munster, each with four seats, and Connacht/Ulster, which has three seats.

The presidential election involves the filling of just one seat and, in the context of this election, it is of assistance to view the whole country as a large one-seat constituency. However, PR-STV really only operates in a presidential election when there are three or more candidates. The process in a two-candidate presidential race is similar to that which would prevail under any other electoral system.

It should also be noted that PR-STV is used for all Dáil by-elections, even though in the case of by-elections, the Dáil constituency where the vacancy occurs becomes a one-seat constituency.[4]

Marking the ballot paper

Whereas proportional representation systems are common throughout the world, our particular type of electoral system with single transferable votes is somewhat rare.

The voter indicates the order of his preference by writing the number 1 opposite the name of his first choice and, if he wishes, the number 2 after his second choice, the number 3 opposite the name of his third choice, and so on. In this way the voter instructs the returning officer that when that vote is being counted, it should be transferred to the second choice candidate if the first choice candidate is either elected or eliminated. If the second choice candidate has also been elected or eliminated, the vote may be transferred to the third choice candidate, and so on.

Arrangements for the count

The returning officer is responsible for conducting the count and making arrangements for it in every constituency.

For Dáil and European elections, the ballot boxes are taken to a central counting centre in each constituency. In the case of European election, the ballot boxes may be opened and the initial sorting of ballot papers may be done at Dáil constituency level prior to transmitting them to the Euro-constituency count centre. For presidential elections and referenda, the votes are counted in each Dáil constituency and the results are transmitted to the national count centre. Not less than four days before polling the returning officer must give written notice to each candidate of the place where the count is to be held and the time at which it will commence. The returning officer is legally required to ensure that, where practicable, the count centre is accessible to persons with physical disabilities.

For Dáil, presidential and local elections the counting of votes takes

---

4.   See Chapter 2 on Constituencies and Electoral Boundaries for a consideration of the procedure and criteria involved in fixing Dáil and European constituencies and local electoral areas.

place at 9 am on the day after polling. The European election result cannot be announced until polling is finished in all Member States; this could be up to three days after the poll has closed in Ireland.[5]

Where two elections or an election and a referendum have been held on the same day, all ballot boxes will be opened and all ballot papers sorted before the count for either poll is conducted.[6] Even though different ballot boxes may be used and different colour ballot papers are used for each poll, all ballot boxes will be open and sorted in order to ensure that the ballot papers for the different polls have not been mixed up.

The Electoral Act 1992 requires that, once begun, the count should so far as practicable continue unbroken, except for breaks for refreshments. The count should not continue past 11 pm or recommence before 9 am unless both the returning officer and candidates agree. In reality, returning officers will continue beyond 11 pm where the count is likely to be completed at a reasonable hour, or to have reached a convenient point to adjourn.

At all times, including periods when counting is suspended, the returning officer must retain the ballot papers in his care 'under his own seal' and must ensure that they are not interfered with.[7]

Agents for candidates at the count
Candidates or their election agents are allowed to attend at the counting of votes. The returning officer decides how many agents each candidate may appoint to be present at the count. The candidate must notify the returning officer at least two days before polling of the names of the agents so appointed.[8]

Although conducted 'in public', before the media, access to the count is restricted to the returning officer's staff, gardaí, and those duly appointed agents for the candidates and others only with the express permission of the returning officer.[9]

The returning officer is required by law to give the agents of the candidate all such reasonable facilities and information as are required to oversee the counting of votes and, in particular, facilities for satisfying themselves that the ballot papers have been sorted correctly.

---

5. See Chapter 4 on Organisation of the Poll.
6. To date, European elections have been held in Ireland on Thursdays/Fridays and the votes have been counted on the following Sunday, with the results announced that evening.
7. See the section on special arrangements where two polls are held on the same date in Chapter 4.
8. For a judicial consideration of this obligation, see *Dillon-Leetch v Calleary*, page 156.
9. For a judicial view on the role of these agents, see *Sherwin v Minister for the Environment* at page 172.

Opening postal votes

As the returned postal votes are received, in the covering envelope provided, the returning officer puts them into the postal voters' ballot boxes. These are opened at some stage before the count begins. Candidates are entitled to appoint agents on their behalf to be present at the opening of the postal ballots.

Each ballot box is opened and the number of envelopes counted. Each covering envelope is then opened in clear view of the attending agents. The receipt or declaration of identity is checked to ensure it is signed. If the declaration of identity is not signed, or if the ballot paper is not accompanied by the required declaration of identify, it is deemed rejected. The returning officer can, however, accept votes as valid even if the ballot paper or declaration of identity is in the wrong envelope, the ballot paper is not in a sealed envelope, or the documents are not returned in the covering envelope.

The sealed envelopes are mixed and opened and the ballot papers, still folded, are placed in a new ballot box. This ballot box is then sealed and is reopened at the count with all the other ballot papers.

Opening the ballot boxes

In normal circumstances, each ballot box is opened and emptied in the presence of agents for the candidates.

As the votes are counted, they must be kept face upwards in order to prevent anyone from seeing the numbers printed on the back of the ballot papers, and so that they are open to scrutiny conveniently to assist tallypersons, who require a clear view of how the papers are marked. Candidates or their agents are not allowed to handle ballot papers during the count.

The next step is to ascertain the total number of ballot papers in each box in order to reconcile it with the number of ballot papers issued at the polling station as notified in the account returned by the relevant presiding officer.

The ballot papers are then mixed thoroughly and sorted into bundles according to the first preference recorded for each candidate. At this stage ballot papers that may be invalid or spoilt are set aside for further scrutiny and accepted or rejected as appropriate. The returning officer calculates the total valid poll by disregarding the spoiled or invalid ballot papers and counting the number of ballot papers in each bundle.

Spoilt or invalid votes

Section 118 of the Electoral Act 1992 defines an invalid vote in the following terms:

- Any ballot paper that does not bear the official mark. The Department of the Environment publishes specific guidelines as to what constitutes the presence of an official mark.[10]

- A ballot paper on which the number 1 or word 'one' or any other mark which might, in the opinion of the returning officer, clearly indicate a first preference is not placed at all or is not placed in such a way as to indicate a preference for one candidate. It follows therefore that even if a number or mark is theoretically capable of expressing a first preference, but is not put opposite, near or connected to a specific candidate it is impossible to determine who it is a vote for and so it is invalid.

- A ballot paper where the number 1 or word 'one' or any other mark which, in the opinion of the returning officer, expresses a preference is set opposite the name of more than one candidate.

- Any ballot paper which has anything written or marked on it (apart from an indicated preference) which, in the opinion of the returning officer, is calculated to identify the voter.

The returning officer must write 'rejected' clearly on any ballot paper, which he deems to be invalid. Where he admits a ballot paper about which there may be a doubt, he can write his reasons for admitting it on the paper in such a way as not to interfere with the voting preferences on it.

It is important to note that the writing of something other than a mark or number or word designed to indicate a voting preference on the ballot paper does not of itself render the vote invalid. The writing, for example, of a political slogan or remark on the ballot paper does not render that vote invalid provided that the slogan or remark is not calculated to identify the voter and that a clear voting preference is otherwise marked on the ballot paper.

Although the clearest way to indicate a first preference is to mark the ballot paper with the word one or number 1, any mark, which in the opinion of the returning officer clearly indicates a preference for one and only one candidate, will be counted as a first preference. The 1992 Act gave the returning officer greater discretion in determining whether or not a ballot paper is valid.

---

10. See section 89, Electoral Act 1992.

Transferable and non-transferable ballot papers

A transferable ballot paper is one on which, following a first preference, a second or subsequent preference is recorded in consecutive numerical order for a remaining candidate. A remaining candidate is one who has not already been deemed elected or eliminated.

Section 118 also defines what amounts to a non-transferable ballot as one of the following:

- A ballot paper on which no second or subsequent preference is recorded for a remaining candidate.

- A ballot paper on which the names of two or more candidates, whether remaining candidates or not, are marked with a mark which, in the opinion of the returning officer, indicates the same preference and are next in order of preference is deemed a non-transferable ballot paper. For example, if on the second count a ballot paper has the number 2 opposite two different candidates, it is non-transferable.

- A ballot paper where the candidate next in order of preference, whether remaining or not, is marked with a mark which, in the opinion of the returning officer, does not follow consecutively after some other mark on the ballot paper.

- A ballot paper that is void for uncertainty.

Calculating the quota

The quota is the minimum number of votes necessary to guarantee the election of a candidate. The quota is ascertained by dividing the total valid poll by one more than the number of seats to be filled in that constituency and adding one to the result. Any fractional remainder is disregarded.

$$\left[\frac{\text{Total Valid Poll}}{\text{Number of candidates} + 1} \right] + 1$$

The calculation can be illustrated with the following example. If 1,000 valid votes are cast in a four-seat constituency the quota is 201.

$$\frac{1,000}{(4+1)} = 200 \qquad 200 + 1 = 201$$

Using this method, only the same number of candidates as there are seats to be filled could reach the quota in any constituency. In the above example of a four-seat constituency, only four candidates could possibly reach the quota.

Deeming a candidate elected

Candidates are deemed elected in one of three circumstances:

- When at the end of any count, the number of votes credited to any candidate is equal to or greater than the quota.

- When the number of remaining candidates equals the remaining number of vacant seats.

- When one seat remains vacant and the candidate has votes greater than the sum of all other remaining candidates plus any undistributed surpluses.

Distribution of surpluses

A surplus is the total number of votes exceeding the quota, which a candidate has following his election. These surplus votes are transferred proportionately to the remaining candidates in the following way.

Surplus on the first count
Where a candidate exceeds the quota on the first count, all of the votes are 'original votes', i.e. first preferences.

All of the votes in the candidate's bundle are examined, and all of those that are transferable (i.e. a subsequent preference is expressed thereon) are arranged into sub-bundles in accordance with the next available preference on them. If the number of transferable votes is equal to or greater than the surplus then each remaining candidate will receive all the votes from the appropriate bundle of transferable papers.

Surpluses on second and subsequent counts
In this instance the votes credited to a candidate are made up of 'original' votes and 'transferred' votes (i.e. his own first preferences and any transfers he has received), or only of transferred votes (if he got no first preferences).

The returning officer examines only those votes in the bundle of transfers last received by the candidate and arranges the transferable votes in that last bundle into further sub-bundles in accordance with the next available preference recorded on them.

If the surplus is exactly equal to the number of transferable votes, which is unlikely, the returning officer simply transfers each of the sub-bundles of transferable votes to the candidate for which the next available preference is stated.

If the surplus is greater than the total number of transferable papers, the ballots in the sub-parcel are transferred directly, and the difference between the total number of transferable papers and the surplus is deemed non-transferable.

If, as is more likely, the surplus is less than the total number of transferable papers, each remaining candidate will receive from the appropriate bundle of transferable papers a number of votes calculated as follows.

$$\frac{\text{Surplus x number of papers in bundle}}{\text{Total number of transferable papers}}$$

Order in which surpluses must be distributed
If two or more candidates exceed the quota on any one count, the larger surplus must be distributed first.

Where two or more candidates have surpluses from two different counts, the surplus of the candidate who exceeded the quota in the earliest count is distributed first.

Where the surplus of the two candidates is exactly the same, the surplus of the candidate who got the most first preferences is distributed first. If the first preferences were equal, then lots are drawn as to which candidate's surplus is distributed first.

A returning officer must transfer the surplus of a candidate deemed elected in all cases except when the surplus, together with any other surpluses not transferred is less than the number of votes the highest remaining candidate needs to reach the quota.

Elimination of candidates

If no candidate has a surplus or the surplus is insufficient to elect one of the remaining candidates or to materially affect the progress of the count, the lowest of the remaining candidates is eliminated and his ballot papers are transferred to remaining candidates according to the next preference indicated on them. If the lowest candidates have equal votes, the one who got the lowest first preference vote is eliminated first. If they have an equal number of first preference votes, lots are drawn to determine which candidate is to be eliminated first.

The returning officer can eliminate two or more of the lowest candidates together where the total votes for all those candidates and any surpluses not transferred is less than the votes of the next highest candidate.

The ability to eliminate candidates together is subject to the protection that one of them either already has or could not otherwise attain one-quarter of a quota. This benchmark entitles them to retain their deposit and qualify for a reimbursement from the Exchequer of some election expenses.[11]

Filling the final seats

When the number of remaining candidates is the same as the number of seats to be filled, the remaining candidates are deemed elected.

Where there is only one seat left to be filled and the highest remaining candidate has more votes than the total of all the other remaining candidates and any surpluses not transferred, the highest remaining candidate is deemed elected.

If any of the remaining candidates does not yet have one-quarter of the quota, which is unlikely, then any further transfer of votes must be carried out in case they would give the remaining candidate enough votes to save his deposit.

Re-counts

It is important to clarify what is involved when a re-count takes place in an election. A re-count does not involve remixing all the ballot papers and restarting the counting of votes. It involves the re-examination of all the bundles that were created by the original counts and rechecking to ensure they were counted and calculated properly. When re-counting, the order of the papers in the bundles and sub-bundles must not be disturbed unless it is necessary to do so, due to the discovery of an error.

Where a significant error is discovered, which is likely to affect the result of the election, the returning officer must count all the papers afresh from the point at which the error occurred.[12]

A candidate or the election agent of a candidate may at the conclusion of any count request a re-examination and re-count of papers dealt with during that count and can request a complete re-examination and re-count of all parcels once and once only. The returning officer is not obliged to, but may grant more than one request for such a re-count.

A returning officer may on his own initiative re-count all or any of the papers at any stage of a count, as often as he wishes, until he is satisfied with to the accuracy of the count.

---

11. See Chapter 14 on Exchequer Funding of Political Parties and Reimbursement of Candidate Election Expenses.

The returning officer has discretion to refuse any request for a recount, which in the returning officer's opinion is frivolous or vexatious or when the parcel has already been re-examined or re-counted.

If, during the course of a re-count being carried out at the request of a candidate, the request is withdrawn, it is at the returning officer's discretion whether or not to continue with the re-count.

Challenging decisions of the returning officer

The returning officer has the final decision on the elimination of a candidate, the admissibility of a vote or the allocation of transfers. Decisions of the returning officer, whether expressed or implied, are final and are subject to reversal only on an election petition to the High Court questioning the election result.[13]

Retention and destruction of ballot papers

On the completion of the count the returning officer must place in separate sealed packs:

- the counted ballot papers;

- the ballot papers rejected at the counting of the votes;

- the unused and spoiled ballot papers,

- the counterfoils of ballot papers issued at polling stations;

- the marked copies of the register of electors;

- the ballot paper accounts;

- the candidate nomination papers (valid and invalid);

- the authorisation to electors to vote at other polling stations.

He marks each sealed pack with the election, the date of polling day and the constituency and forwards them to the Clerk of the Dáil.

The Clerk of the Dáil retains all these documents for six months from the date of the poll at the election. The documents cannot be inspected by anyone except by order of the High Court. The High Court can only make

---

13. See Chapter 18 on Election and Referendum Petitions. For a consideration on who can call a re-count and on the necessity for candidates to be given 'a considerable pause', to decide whether they wish to call a re-count see *Byrne v Allen and Others,* page 153.

such an order for the purposes of an election petition or where the inspection or production of the documents is required for the purpose of instituting or maintaining a prosecution for an offence under the electoral acts. If such an order is not made or unless he has reason to believe that the papers will be required for such purposes, the Clerk of the Dáil, after the six months have passed, must arrange for all these documents (including the ballot papers) to be destroyed.

7 Seanad Elections

The composition of the Seanad

Article 18 of the Constitution provides that the Seanad, or Upper House of the Oireachtas, shall be composed of 60 members.[1] In contrast to the situation as regards Dáil membership, the number of senators is fixed, and there is no provision for alterations to take account of adjustments in population.

The 60 Seanad members acquire their membership in three different ways. Eleven members are not elected, but are appointed by the Taoiseach of the day. Six members are elected by university graduates – three by graduates of the National University of Ireland and three by graduates of the University of Dublin (Trinity College Dublin). The remaining 43 senators are elected from five "vocational panels" by TDs, senators and members of county councils and the five county borough councils.

The calling of Seanad elections

The Constitution links the calling of Seanad elections to the dissolution of the Dáil. Article 18.8 provides that a Seanad election must take place not later than 90 days after a dissolution of the Dáil and that the first meeting of the new Seanad shall take place on a day to be fixed by the President on the advice of the Taoiseach.[2]

However, the outgoing Seanad remains in existence, and members continue to be senators, until "the day before polling day" for the new Seanad. 'Polling day' is not defined in the Constitution but is generally taken to mean the last date upon which electors can vote. The outgoing Seanad can continue to sit and enact legislation during the period from the dissolution of the old Dáil right up to the election of the new Seanad.

A constitutional anomaly exists whereby it is possible that a newly elected Dáil could be dissolved and a second general election called before the new Seanad is elected. This would necessitate another Seanad election

---

1. See page 182
2. For the law relating to the election of members of the Seanad, see generally, the Seanad Electoral (Panel Members) Act 1947, the Seanad Electoral (Panel Members) Act 1954 and the Seanad Electoral (University Members) Act 1937.

and give rise to what Professor John Kelly called the "absurdity" of two Seanad elections in quick succession.[3] Although this situation would be no more absurd than the associated two Dáil elections in succession, a report from the Constitutional Review Group recommends closing this anomaly by providing that the originally occasioned Seanad election should be aborted and an election related to the second Dáil dissolution should be held in its place.

Eligibility for election to the Seanad

The Constitution provides that in order to be eligible for election or nomination to the Seanad, an individual must be eligible for election to the Dáil. A candidate must be at least 21 years old and the same constitutional incapacities and legal disqualifications apply.[4]

The electoral system

The Constitution also provides that the election of members on the university or "vocational" panels must be by proportional representation with a single transferable vote (PR-STV). Voting must be conducted by secret postal vote.

The university panels

The National University of Ireland and the University of Dublin each elect three members of the Seanad. The provision for Seanad seats for the National University of Ireland and the University of Dublin is to be found in Article 18.4 of the 1937 Constitution. The two universities had three Dáil seats under the 1922 Constitution; these were abolished in the 1937 Constitution.

In 1979, a constitutional amendment was passed by referendum inserting a new subsection into Article 18.4.[5] It provides for the election by universities and other institutions of higher education specified by law of such number of members of Seanad Éireann, not exceeding six, as may be specified by law. Those elected would replace the six senators currently elected by the National University of Ireland and the University of Dublin (Trinity College). Despite various indications of an intention to extend the franchise and the number of third-level institutions whose graduates might participate in Seanad elections, the Oireachtas has, to date, failed to give legislative effect to this 1979 amendment.

The electorate for the university seats is limited to graduates who are

---

3. See John Kelly, *The Irish Constitution* (Butterworths, 2nd edn.)
4. See Eligibility for Membership in Chapter 5 on Dáil Elections.
5. See page 183.

Irish citizens and who have reached 18 years of age. The awarding of a
graduate or undergraduate degree (but not an honorary degree) entitles one
to a vote. In the University of Dublin constituency, certain scholarship
holders are also entitled to vote. A person can only have one vote in a university constituency, even if they have more than one degree from that university. However, if a person has a degree from each of the two universities then he or she is entitled to a vote in both the National University of
Ireland and University of Dublin constituencies.

University constituencies – poll and count

The register of electors for each university is maintained by that university's governing body. A decision not to register a person who believes they
are entitled to vote can be appealed to the Circuit Court. The returning officers are the vice-chancellor of the National University of Ireland and the
provost of Trinity College Dublin.

Any person over 18 who is qualified for membership of the Seanad can
be nominated to contest the election on a university panel. The person need
not be a graduate of the university and need not in fact be a graduate at all.
Candidates are nominated in writing by ten registered electors of the university. Party political affiliation is not included on ballot papers for
Seanad elections.

Ballot papers are posted to graduates at their registered address.
Graduates must complete a statutory declaration of identity. When the ballot paper is completed, it is put in a sealed envelope. This sealed envelope,
together with the statutory declaration that must be witnessed by another
person, is inserted into another envelope and returned by post to the returning officer. The election is by PR-STV and the count is conducted in each
university as it would be conducted in any three-seat constituency.[6]

The vocational panels

Article 18.4 provides that 43 Seanad members will be elected from vocational panels, and Article 18.7.2° provides that not more than eleven and not
less than five members of the Seanad shall be elected from any one panel.[7]

There are currently five such vocational panels. Each vocational panel
is further divided into two sub-panels.

- The Oireachtas sub-panel contains the name of each candidate
  nominated by members of the Oireachtas. Each candidate must be

---

6. The count in this instance is the same as in Dáil or European constituencies, see gen-
    erally Chapter 6 on Electoral System and the Count.
7. See generally Seanad Electoral (Panel Members) Act 1947.

nominated in writing by at least four members of the Oireachtas, i.e. the incoming Dáil and the outgoing Seanad. Each Oireachtas member can only be party to the nomination of one candidate.

- The nominating bodies sub-panel includes the name of each candidate nominated by bodies on the register of nominating bodies.

The vocational panel nominating bodies

A register of nominating bodies for each panel is maintained and revised annually by the Clerk of the Seanad. In order to be eligible to be registered to nominate candidates on a vocational panel, a body must:

- have objects that relate to the interest or services relevant to that panel; or

- represent people who have knowledge and practical experience of the area relevant to the panel.

The current register of nominating bodies contains a range of social, charitable, academic and professional bodies, as well as trade unions. The number of nominating bodies varies for each panel.

At present, the number of members elected from each panel, the minimum number which must be elected from each sub-panel and the interests and areas represented by each panel are as follows:

- five members from the cultural and educational panel (representing the national language and culture, literature, art, education, law and medicine, including surgery, dentistry, veterinary medicine and pharmaceutical chemistry) of whom two at least are elected from each sub-panel;

- eleven members from the agricultural panel (representing agriculture and allied interests and fisheries) of whom four at least are elected from each sub-panel;

- eleven members from the labour panel (representing labour, whether organised or unorganised), of whom four at least are elected from each sub-panel;

- nine members from the industrial and commercial panel (representing industry and commerce and including banking, finance, accountancy, engineering and architecture) of whom three at least are elected from each sub-panel;

- seven members from the administrative panel (representing public administration and social services, including voluntary social activities) of whom three at least are elected from each sub-panel.

Adjudication on nominations for the vocational panels

In order to be nominated on any of the panels, a person must satisfy the returning officer that he or she has "knowledge and practical experience in the interest or service" of the area relevant to that panel.

After the close of nominations on a day appointed by ministerial order, the returning officer sits with a judicial assessor – a judge of the High Court – to adjudicate on the nominations. A question relating to a person's eligibility for nomination because of statutory incapacity or disqualification may be referred to the judicial assessor for his decision on the point of law involved, and the returning officer then decides whether the nomination is in order.

The question of "knowledge and interest" of a certain vocational sector was ruled on by the High Court in *Ormonde v MacGabhann*.[8] In this case, a candidate sought a nomination on the labour panel. The court held that a candidate must have a reasonable amount of knowledge of the problems that arise in our society between employees and employers. It further held that, if the candidate had a reasonable amount of practical experience with these problems, this was sufficient to qualify them for the labour panel. However, Pringle J. held that mere membership of a trade union would not of itself be sufficient.

Vocational panel electorate

The electorate for the vocational panels is made up of:

- members of the incoming Dáil elected in the general election;

- members of the outgoing Seanad;

- members of every county council and the five county borough councils, namely the corporations of Dublin, Cork, Waterford, Galway and Limerick.

If a person is a member of more than one of those categories, their name is entered only once on the electoral roll and they are only entitled to one vote on each panel. The full roll of those entitled to vote for the vocational panels is published in *Iris Oifigiúil* prior to the issuing of ballot papers.

---

8. See *Ormonde v MacGabhann*, page 170.

Vocational panel voting arrangements

By law, the returning officer for the Seanad election for "vocational" panels is the Clerk of the Seanad. The returning officer issues, to each voter on the electoral roll, a list of the candidates nominated for each panel and details of the body or persons who nominated them. On the day appointed by ministerial order, the returning officer sends five ballot papers (one for each panel) to each voter by registered post. Each ballot paper lists the candidates for that panel in alphabetical order. Their name, address and description as on the nomination paper are included. The sub-panel from which each candidate is nominated is also included. However, party political affiliations are not included.

The voter must complete a declaration of identity in the presence of an authorised person.[9] The elector then marks each of the ballot papers in order of preference. Each of the five ballot papers must then be put in a separate sealed ballot envelope provided. These five ballot envelopes must be returned with the declaration of identity in a covering envelope by post to the returning officer. Although a voter can leave one or more of the ballot papers unmarked, all five ballot papers must be returned in sealed ballot envelopes in order for that elector's vote on any of the five panels to be deemed valid. If less than five ballot papers are returned, then all that voter's ballots are invalid.

The vocational panel count

The complexities of counting votes under the PR-STV system in multi-seat constituencies are outlined in more detail in Chapter 6 above. In the context of a Seanad election, they are further complicated by the requirement that a minimum number of candidates be elected from each sub-panel within each of the five vocational panels.

A separate count is held for each of the five panels. The votes are usually counted across three or four days in Leinster House. Once the ballot papers have been opened and checked, they are sorted in accordance with the first preference shown on them. To facilitate counting and for ease of calculating transfers, each vote is given a value of 1,000. The appropriate value of first-preference votes is credited to each candidate. The quota is calculated by dividing the total value of valid votes by the number of seats to be filled on that panel plus one and then adding one. For example, if the total number of valid votes cast was 900, the total value of these would be 900,000 and, if there were five seats to be filled on that panel, then the quota would be 150,001.

---

9. For example, the Secretary of a County Council or County Borough Council or the Clerk of the Dáil or Seanad.

$$\frac{900,000}{5+1} = 150,000 \qquad 150,000+1 = 150,001$$

It can be seen from the above example that it is only possible for five candidates to reach the quota.

As the value of a candidate's votes equals or exceeds the quota, he is deemed elected unless his election would make the election of the minimum number of members from each sub-panel impossible. In other words, a candidate on one sub-panel may reach the quota but, because his election will result in the minimum number of candidates not being elected from the other sub-panel, he or she is not deemed elected. If a candidate receives more than a quota, the surplus is distributed to the remaining candidates in accordance with the next effective preference shown on the ballot paper concerned.

Where the maximum number of candidates has been elected for a sub-panel, the values of the votes of the remaining candidates on that sub-panel are distributed in accordance with the next effective preference shown on the ballot papers.

If no candidate has a surplus, the lowest candidate is excluded and their votes are distributed at the value at which they were received. However, a candidate cannot be eliminated if their elimination would make the election of the minimum number of members from each sub-panel impossible.

Article 19 provides that legislation may be introduced to enable the direct election – by any functional or vocational group or association or council – of so many members of Seanad Éireann as may be fixed by such law in substitution for an equal number of the members to be elected from the corresponding panels of candidates constituted under the Constitution. The legislature has proved reluctant to activate this constitutional provision.

Declaration of the result

On completion of the count, the returning officers for the university constituencies forward certificates to the Clerk of the Seanad notifying him/her of the names of the candidates elected. The names of the members nominated by the Taoiseach are communicated to the clerk by the Department of the Taoiseach. The members of the new Seanad are notified by the clerk to attend and sign the roll. At the first meeting of the Seanad after the election, the clerk announces the names of the members who have been elected and nominated.

Seanad by-elections

Where a casual vacancy occurs among the members of the Seanad nominated by the Taoiseach, the Cathaoirleach of the Seanad sends a notice of the vacancy to the Taoiseach who then nominates a person to fill the vacancy.

Where a vacancy occurs among the members of the Seanad elected on the vocational panels, the Clerk of the Seanad sends a notice in writing to the Minister for the Environment who makes an order for the holding of a by-election. The Constitution provides that vacancies among the elected members shall be filled in a manner laid out by law.

Section 69 of the Seanad Electoral (Panel Members) Act 1947 provides that the electorate for a Seanad by-election arising from a vacancy on the vocational panel is restricted to members of the Dáil and Seanad only. Councillors (unless of course they are also Oireachtas members) do not vote in by-elections. In the case of a vacancy on an Oireachtas sub-panel, a by-election candidate must be nominated by nine members of the Oireachtas. If the vacancy occurred on the nominating bodies sub-panel, the by-election candidate must be nominated by a registered nominating body relevant to that vocational panel. The count is conducted in the same way as a Seanad general election but without the modification necessary to ensure that a minimum number is elected from each sub-panel.

Vacancies from among the university members are filled by a by-election. In this instance, the nomination procedure, poll and the electorate are the same as those that prevail during a general election by university members.

8 European Elections

Legal framework

The various treaties establishing the European Union provide for the eventual introduction of a uniform electoral system across all Member States to govern elections to the European parliament. Such a common electoral legal framework has not yet been introduced, and the elements of the law governing European elections in each Member State are still to be found in their own national legislation.

In Ireland, the conduct of European elections is governed by European law, Council Decision (76/787/EEC) of 20 September 1976, Council Directive (93/109/EC) of 6 December 1993 and by national legislation, primarily the European Parliament Elections Act 1997.

The minimum legal requirements regarding the right of European citizens to vote and to stand in European Parliament elections are common to all Member States. The Council Directive of 20 September 1976 laid down the initial requirement that members be elected by direct universal suffrage. More recently Council Directive 93/09/EC (6 December 1993) detailed the electoral arrangements for citizens of the European Union who reside in Member States of which they are not nationals and who wish to vote or to stand as candidates in European Parliament elections.

The primary legislation dealing with European elections in Ireland is the European Parliament Elections Act 1997. This must be read in conjunction with the provisions concerning European elections in the Electoral Act 1992 and the European Parliament Election (Voting and Candidature) Regulation 1994. It is important to note that there are no constitutional provisions specifically governing the conduct of European elections in Ireland. It would therefore, for example, be difficult to mount a constitutional challenge to the relevant legislative provisions other than on general equality and proportionality grounds.

Date of European elections

The first direct election of Irish Members of the European Parliament (MEPs) was held in June 1979. Since then, European elections have been held at fixed five-year intervals from that date. It is not necessary that elections are held on the same date in each Member State, rather the elections must take place within a four-day period in the month of June. This four-day period is fixed by the European Council of Ministers. However, the declaration of count results cannot be made until voting has been completed in all Member States.

The exact polling date in Ireland is set by order of the Minister for the Environment, and this order must be made at least 35 days before the election. Traditionally, elections have been held on the second Thursday in June, but the count doesn't begin until the following Sunday. As with Dáil elections, the Minister for the Environment orders the opening hours for the poll. The poll must be open for at least twelve hours between the hours of 8 am and 10.30 pm, and the opening hours must be the same at all polling stations.

European constituencies

The Republic of Ireland currently has the right to elect fifteen members of the European Parliament. They are elected on the basis of the following constituencies:

Connacht-Ulster	3 seats
Dublin	4 seats
Leinster	4 seats
Munster	4 seats

The European constituency boundaries are now fixed by legislation enacted on the recommendations of the statutory constituency commission, which comes into existence after the publication of each national census.[1]

Section 15(2) of the European Parliament Elections Act 1997 provides that the Minister for Environment, having considered any report presented to the Oireachtas by the constituency commission, must submit proposals for the review of the Euro-constituency to the Dáil and the Seanad. In 1998, the commission set up to review both Dáil and European constituencies recommended that there be no change to the boundaries or seat allocation of the European constituencies.

The total number of MEPs that Ireland is entitled to elect can be changed at the European level. Seats are allocated to each Member State on a general pro rata population basis. It is likely that at some future date, as the number of Member States increases and the size of the parliament becomes increasingly unwieldy, a reduction in the size of the Irish representation may be required.

---

1. See Chapter 1 on Constituencies and Electoral Boundaries.

Eligibility to vote

Every Irish citizen or national of another European Union Member State who is resident in Ireland, who is over 18 years of age and whose name appears on the register of electors is entitled to vote in European elections.[2] Entitlements to postal votes and to be registered as special voters are the same as those for other polls. A person only has one vote in each European election and can only be registered to vote in one constituency and only in one Member State.

A national of a Member State, apart from Ireland and the UK, will not be registered unless, in addition to completing a normal application form, they also furnish, to the registration authority, a statutory declaration stating:

- his nationality;

- the address in Ireland at which he is ordinarily resident;

- where applicable, the locality or constituency in which he was last registered in the Member State of which he is a national (home Member State); and

- a declaration that he will exercise his right to vote in Ireland only.

The local registration authority, through the Department of the Environment and Local Government, is obliged to send a copy of this declaration to the elector's home Member State.

In Ireland, the legislation provides that elections to the European Parliament must be by proportional representation with single transferable vote (PR-STV) – the electoral system that is used for Dáil elections. It is worth noting that the electoral system for European elections could be changed – perhaps as part of a move to introduce a uniform electoral system across Europe – without recourse to a constitutional referendum. Legislation also provides that voting in European elections shall be by secret ballot, but again this is a statutory right and not a constitutional right.

Eligibility for election to the European Parliament

Every citizen of Ireland and every national of another Member State who is over 21 on the date of the poll and who is not disqualified by European

---

2. See generally Chapter 2 on Franchise and the Register of Electors.

Community or national law from standing as a candidate in another Member State is eligible to be elected to the European Parliament. A person can only be nominated as a candidate in one constituency in Ireland and cannot be a candidate in Ireland if already nominated as a candidate in another Member State.

Those who are not eligible for election to the European Parliament are:

- a person who has not reached the age of 21 years;

- a person who is not a citizen of Ireland or a national of an EU Member State who is ordinarily resident in the State;

- a national of an EU Member State (other than the UK) who has been deprived, through an individual criminal law or civil law decision, of the right to be a candidate under the law of their home Member State;

- a holder of the office of President of Ireland, minister or minister of state, judge or comptroller and auditor general;

- a member of the Commission of the European Union;

- a judge, advocate general or registrar of the Court of Justice of the European Union;

- a member of the Court of Auditors of the European Union;

- a member of the consultative Committee of the European Coal and Steel Community or member of the Economic and Social Committee of the European Economic Community and of the European Atomic Energy Community;

- a member of a committee set up pursuant to the treaties establishing the European Coal and Steel Community, the European Economic Community and the European Atomic Energy Community for the purpose of managing the communities' funds or carrying out a permanent direct administrative task;

- a member of the board of directors, management committee or staff of the European Investment Bank;

- an active official or servant of the institutions of the European Union or of the specialised bodies attached to them;

- a member of the Garda Síochána;

- a member of the permanent defence forces;

- a civil servant who is not by the terms of their employment express-ly permitted to be a member of the European Parliament;

- a person of unsound mind;

- a person undergoing a sentence of imprisonment for any term exceeding six months imposed by a court of competent jurisdiction in the State;

- an undischarged bankrupt under an adjudication by a court of com-petent jurisdiction in the State.

It should be noted that ordinary members of the Dáil and Seanad are not legally precluded from simultaneously serving as members of the European Parliament and indeed a number of deputies retain the so-called 'dual mandate'. Some political parties now have internal rules prohibiting their Oireachtas members from contesting the European elections or at least requiring an elected member to opt for one parliament or the other at the succeeding general election. However, the office of minister, minister of state or attorney general is incompatible with membership of the European Parliament.

Nomination of candidates
Nominations for European elections are usually made a month before polling day with a seven day period between the opening and closing of nominations. Candidates can nominate themselves or be nominated, with their consent, by another person who is an elector from that constituency.

Candidate deposit
As with Dáil elections, a deposit is required from candidates. The 1997 Act provides that before the close of nominations, the candidate, or someone acting on their behalf, must lodge £1,000 with the returning officer. If this is not done by the close of nominations the candidate is deemed to have withdrawn his or her candidature. The deposit is refunded if the candidate withdraws his candidature, dies before the opening of the polls, is elected, or is not elected but the total number of votes credited to that candidate at any stage of the count exceeds one quarter of the quota.

Candidates who are nationals of another Member State
Any candidate who is a national of a Member State other than Ireland and the United Kingdom must, in addition to completing the normal nomination form, complete a statutory declaration and produce an attestation from his home Member State that he is not disqualified from being a candidate there.

Party affiliation
The party political affiliation of candidates for European elections appears below their name. This will include the name of both the national political party and the European Parliament political group that is noted on the register of political parties in relation to that party. In order to authenticate his or her party affiliation for inclusion on the ballot papers, the candidate must present a "certificate of party affiliation" signed by a national party official as designated on the register of political parties maintained by the Clerk of the Dáil.[3]

Non-party candidates can opt to have the designation "NON PARTY" inserted below their name on the ballot paper or to leave the relevant space blank. A non-party candidate who is a sitting MEP may have the name of any European party political grouping to which he is affiliated inserted after his name, provided that he produces a certificate of European political affiliation signed by a designated member of the secretariat of the relevant political grouping.

Candidate photographs on the ballot paper
Section 2(b) of the European Parliament Elections Act 1997 provides that a ballot paper may include a photograph of each candidate. Photographs of candidates appeared on ballot papers in an election in Ireland for the first time in the June 1999 European election. The European Parliament Election (Forms) Regulation 1998,[4] published in relation to that election, provided that, if a candidate wished to have their photograph included on the ballot paper, they must provide two photographs with the nomination form. The photographs had to be 75mm x 100mm, recently taken, of good quality, in colour and taken to a professional standard, showing the candidate's full face, head and shoulders only on a light background.

If only one copy of the photograph is provided or if the copies produced do not comply with the specifications, the returning officer has the discretion not to include it on the ballot paper. If a candidate does not provide a photograph or if the returning officer decides not to include the photograph

---

3. See section on register of political parties in Chapter 4 on Organisation of the Poll.
4. SI No. 415 of 1998.

provided, the space on the ballot paper intended for that candidate's photograph is left blank.

Replacement candidates

There is no provision for by-elections to the European Parliament. Casual vacancies are filled from lists of replacement candidates that are presented at the election preceding the vacancy. Where a vacancy arises, the replacement is the person who remains at the top of the replacement list and is willing to be an MEP.

A list of nominations for replacement candidates must be presented to the returning officer before the close of nominations. The replacement lists presented by registered political parties may contain up to four names more than the number of candidates presented by that party in that constituency. The replacement list of a non-party candidate may contain up to three names.

In order to qualify for nomination as a replacement candidate, one must be eligible for election as a member of the European Parliament, and the same disqualifications and exclusions apply to replacement candidates. A person cannot be nominated as a replacement candidate in respect of more than one constituency.

The entry on the ballot paper for each candidate contains a reference to the associated replacement list. A person who is a candidate in a European Parliament election can also be listed as a replacement candidate. Accordingly, it is usual for the parties to put the candidates on the replacement list so that any of the candidates who are not elected will be eligible to fill any casual vacancies that arise for the party representation for that constituency. The lists of replacement candidates are published by the returning officer, and copies of the lists are displayed in each polling station.

As mentioned, a vacancy is filled by the person on the relevant replacement list who is both eligible and willing to become an MEP. If no replacement candidate list was presented in respect of the MEP who originally won the seat, the list is exhausted or no one remaining on the list is both eligible and willing to become an MEP, Dáil Éireann may select a person to fill the vacancy from the replacement candidates' list presented for the constituency at the election one previous to that again.

Returning officers and the organisation of the poll

The Minister for the Environment appoints a returning officer for each of the European constituencies. This must be the registrar (or sheriff) for one of the county or county boroughs within that European constituency. The returning officer is responsible for the overall organisation of the poll and the conduct of the count in that Euro-constituency. The Dáil returning officers in each county or county borough assist as local returning officers by organising the polling arrangements in each county or county borough area. The arrangements for the conduct of the poll, the polling scheme, the issuing of ballot papers and the conduct of the count are the same as for Dáil elections and are dealt with in more detail in other chapters.[5]

Declaration of the result

On completion of the count, the returning officer declares the result of the election and forwards the names of the elected members to the chief returning officer who notifies the European Parliament.

5. See Chapter 4 on Organisation of the Poll and Chapter 6 on Electoral System and the Count.

9 Presidential Elections

The Constitution provides for the direct election of the President of Ireland. Given that, with the exception of a small number of important powers, the role of the Irish President is limited and largely ceremonial, a direct election is unusual. In most other countries where the role of the President is predominantly ceremonial, presidents are elected by parliament or by an electoral college.

The law governing presidential elections in Ireland is to be found in Article 12 of the Constitution[1] and in the Electoral Act 1992, the Presidential Elections Act 1993, the Electoral (Amendment) Act 1996 and the Electoral Act 1997

Date of presidential election

The President's full term of office is seven years. If the outgoing President is serving a full term, the presidential election must take place 60 days before the expiration of her term of office.

It is possible that an outgoing President's term may come to an end prematurely, whether by death, resignation or impeachment or where she has been deemed permanently incapacitated and where such incapacity has been established to the satisfaction of the Supreme Court. In these circumstances, a presidential election must be held within 60 days after the occurrence of the vacancy.

The Minister for the Environment makes an order in the usual manner setting the polling day and the period for voting, which must last for at least twelve hours between 8 am and 10.30 pm. Legislative provision is made for changing the date of the presidential election date in circumstances where the Dáil has been dissolved.[2] Even if the ministerial order has already been made, the presidential election date can be amended to coincide with the general election date if desired.

The electoral system and eligibility to vote

The Constitution provides that the President must be elected by secret bal-

---

1. See page 178.
2. Electoral Act 1992 as amended.

lot and by (PR-STV) proportional representation with single transferable vote.[3] The form of the ballot paper is prescribed by law and, as is the case in all other elections, the names of the candidates appear in alphabetical order. In contrast to Dáil and European elections, no political affiliations appear on ballot papers for presidential elections

Every citizen of Ireland who is ordinarily resident in the State, is at least 18 years old and whose name is entered on the register of electors is entitled to vote.[4] Nationals of the United Kingdom or other European Union Member States, even if ordinarily resident in Ireland, are not entitled to vote in presidential elections.

Eligibility for election to the office of President
The Constitution provides that any citizen of Ireland who has reached her 35th year is eligible to be President of Ireland. There is a discrepancy between the Irish and English versions of the constitutional text on this point. The English language version of Article 12.4.1° states that one must have reached one's 35th year, whereas the Irish language version requires that one have completed one's 35th year. The Irish language variation of the text would prevail should the issue ever be significant, as Article 25.5.4° of the Constitution stipulates that, where there is a conflict between the two texts, the Irish version shall prevail.[5]

The age limit has attracted some criticism on the grounds that it should be left to the electorate to decide whether a person has the necessary maturity to hold the position. Interestingly, the Constitutional Review Group in 1997 argued against changing the age requirement, while the Oireachtas Joint Committee on the Constitution recommended that it should be reduced to coincide with the age limit for Dáil and Seanad members, which stands at 21.

The requirement that candidates be citizens of Ireland is consistent with that in most countries but, interestingly, does not go as far as requiring that candidates be born in the State, as is required, for example, of candidates for the American presidency.

Apart from the age and citizenship requirements, the Constitution does not permit the Oireachtas to impose any disqualification or ineligibility on potential candidates for the office. The Constitution does not disqualify persons of unsound mind or those serving a prison sentence from contesting a presidential election. Although a range of officers, including judges,

---

3. See generally Chapter 6 on Electoral System and the Count.
4. See Chapter 2 on Franchise and the Register of Electors.
5. See John Kelly, *The Irish Constitution*, (Butterworths, 3rd edn) p. 210.

are prohibited from contesting Dáil elections, there is no requirement that a candidate who holds such a position resign from it before contesting a presidential election.

The outgoing president or any former president who has served only one term is eligible for re-election to the presidency, but only once. Interestingly, even a former or outgoing president who has resigned or who has been impeached and who has only served one term can be nominated or nominate herself to contest a further presidential election.

Any TD or Senator can be a candidate in a presidential election. However, once elected President, she is deemed automatically to have vacated her seat in the Dáil or Seanad. The Constitution also requires that once a successful presidential candidate has taken up office, she shall not hold any other office or position of emolument.

Returning officers and organisation of the poll

A presidential returning officer oversees the nomination process and the conduct of a presidential election where necessary. The presidential returning officer is nominated by order of the Minister for the Environment. In recent elections, the principal officer heading up the franchise section in the Department of Environment has been nominated to be the presidential returning officer. The opening and closing dates for the receipt of nominations are also set by ministerial order.

For the purpose of a presidential election, the country is divided into the same constituencies as for a Dáil election. The Dáil returning officer for a constituency (i.e. the sheriff or county registrar) is the local returning officer for the constituency.

Nomination of candidates

The Constitution provides that a candidate for the presidency can be nominated in one of three ways.

Self renomination

An outgoing or former president who has served only one term can renominate herself. This option was most recently exercised by Patrick Hillery who, although nominated by Fianna Fail in 1976, opted to nominate himself for his unopposed second term in 1983. The facility for self renomination is designed to enable a former president to remain "above party politics" should she seek a second term. In this instance, the nomination paper must be signed by the candidate herself and returned to the presidential returning officer.

Nomination by members of the Oireachtas

A candidate for the presidency can be nominated by not less than twenty members of the Oireachtas. Each Oireachtas member can only support the nomination of one candidate and must be a member of the Oireachtas on the date of nomination, not necessarily on the date of the presidential election. If an Oireachtas member does happen to sign more than one nomination paper, the first received by the presidential returning officer is deemed to be the valid one.

Nomination by county and county borough councils

A candidate can be nominated by four county or county borough councils. This innovative constitutional provision had remained dormant for over 60 years due in no small way to the controls held over the membership of county and county borough councils by the various political parties. However, the provision came to life in the 1997 presidential election when two of the five candidates in that election were nominated by county councils. It is likely to remain a feature of future presidential election nominations.

Each council can support the nomination of one candidate only. The nomination is made by the passage of a resolution by the council by simple majority. The Presidential Elections Act 1993 requires that notice of the intention to propose such a nomination resolution must be given to every member of the council at least three days in advance. The nomination paper must be sealed with the seal of the council and delivered to the presidential returning officer.

There has been some criticism of the mechanism for nominating a presidential candidate on the grounds that it is limited and too narrow. In *Lennon v Minister for the Environment*,[6] it was argued that the provisions of the Constitution were contrary to the common good in that they gave elected politicians an unfair hold over the choice available to the people. The plaintiff's application for an injunction to halt that year's presidential election was rejected. Lennon's case pre-dated the expression of local authority activism which gave rise to the nominations of Rosemary (Dana) Scallan and Derek Nally by local authorities in 1997, which has opened the possibility of a broader range of candidates in future. There have been sustained calls for an even broader mechanism for popular nomination of a presidential candidate, whether by a petition of voters or otherwise.

---

6. See The Irish Times, 24 November 1990.

Adjudication of nominations

At 12 noon on the last day for receiving nominations, the presidential returning officer rules, together with a judicial assessor, on the validity of the nominations. The judicial assessor must be the President of the High Court or another High Court judge nominated by the President of the High Court. Every prospective candidate or her authorised representative must attend at the ruling on nominations and must furnish all relevant information required by the presidential returning officer or the judicial assessor.

The presidential returning officer is required to object to the description of a candidate, which is, in his opinion, incorrect, insufficient to identify the candidate or unnecessarily long. The candidate, her authorised representative or the presidential returning officer may amend the particulars shown on the nomination paper. A candidate may appeal to the High Court against the presidential returning officer's ruling on the validity of a nomination or on the eligibility of her own candidature or that of any other candidate.

Nominations must be on a prescribed nomination form and must be delivered to the presidential returning officer within a prescribed period. A candidate may withdraw at any time up to the close of the ruling on nominations.

Where only one candidate is nominated

The Constitution provides that no election is necessary if only one candidate is nominated. This has been the situation on five occasions to date. The 1993 Act sets out that in circumstances where, at the close of nominations, only one person stands nominated the presidential returning officer declares that person elected, notifies the Taoiseach and publishes the declaration in *Iris Oifigiúil*.

Where no candidate is nominated

If no candidate stands nominated at the close of nominations, the nomination process must commence all over again. Similarly, where any candidate dies after the close of nominations and before the polling date, the returning officer must cancel the poll and recommence the nomination procedure.

The count and the declaration of results

The arrangement and conduct of the count is similar to that for other polls, as outlined at Chapter 6 above, with the following differences. The votes are counted in the individual constituencies, and the results are then forwarded to the presidential returning officer at a national count centre. In normal circumstances, the count commences at 9 am on the day after polling day. Each candidate is entitled to be represented at the counting of the votes and may demand a partial or complete re-count of all the ballot papers.

As in other polls, each ballot box is opened and the number of ballot papers checked against a return furnished by the presiding officer. The papers are sorted according to the first preferences shown on them, and the number of first preference votes recorded for each candidate is notified to the presidential returning officer at the national count centre. That officer calculates the quota (the number of votes necessary for election). With a single position to be filled, the quota is 50 per cent of the valid votes plus one. If a candidate receives a number of votes equal to or greater than the quota, he/she is declared elected.

If no candidate reaches the quota, the presidential returning officer directs the local returning officers in each constituency to exclude the lowest candidate, transfer her votes in accordance with the next preference shown on them and notify the presidential returning officer of the result. The two or more lowest candidates must be excluded together where the sum of their votes is less than the votes of the next lowest candidate. The process of excluding candidates and transferring their votes continues until one of the candidates has sufficient votes to secure election. That candidate is then declared elected by the presidential returning officer.

10 Local Elections

Legal framework

Local government and local elections in Ireland were given constitutional recognition for the first time following a referendum in June 1999.[1] This constitutional amendment, together with the Local Government Act 1994, provides the general framework for the conduct of local elections. The detailed provisions regarding the nomination of candidates, the organisation of the poll and the conduct of the count are set out in the Local Elections Regulation 1995. The scheme for local elections is generally similar to that set out for Dáil elections in the Electoral Act 1992. To this end, the law governing local elections can be taken to be the same as that for Dáil elections except where specified in this chapter.[2]

Local Authorities

The term 'local elections' is a generic description incorporating elections to county councils, corporations of county boroughs, urban district councils and town commissions. County councils are responsible for local government in the 29 administrative counties.[3] County borough corporations (generally known as corporations) are responsible for local government in the cities of Dublin, Cork, Galway, Limerick and Waterford. Borough corporations and urban district councils have certain local government functions in the larger towns. Town commissioners have limited functions in 26 smaller towns. A reference to 'council' in this chapter can be taken to incorporate all of these councils unless otherwise stated.

Date of local elections

Historically, there was a requirement that local elections be held every five

---

1. Twentieth Amendment of the Constitution, passed by referendum June 1999.
2. For law relevant to local elections generally, in addition to the Electoral Act 1992 see Local Government Act 1941 (Part IV), Local Elections (Petitions and Disqualifications) Act 1974, Local Government Act 1994, Local Elections Regulation 1995, Electoral (Amendment) Act 1996 and Electoral Act 1997.
3. There are 26 geographical counties, but the county of Tipperary is divided into two administrative counties and the county of Dublin is divided into three administrative counties.

years. In recent decades, this time limit was repeatedly extended by the passage of a resolution or amending legislation by the Oireachtas.

The Local Government Act 1994 provided that a local election be held every five years in the month of June, but this was overridden by amending legislation in 1996, which postponed the election due to be held that year.

The requirements governing the holding of local elections were given a constitutional basis, and placed beyond the legislature's reach, in the referendum on local government in June 1999. The Constitution now provides specifically that elections for members of local authorities must be held not later than the end of the fifth year after the year in which they were last held.

Local electoral areas and the designation of aldermen

The 1994 Act gives the Minister for the Environment the power to divide a council area into local electoral areas, to set the borders of these electoral areas and to fix the number of members to be elected for each electoral area. The 38 larger local authorities are divided into two or more local electoral areas.[4]

There is a historical practice whereby certain members of a corporation are deemed senior councillors ranking next to the mayor in importance. Although the effect of the designation of alderman in modern times is largely ceremonial, it does exist and the Act gives the minister the power to specify the number of aldermen for each corporation of a county borough and the number to be elected in each electoral area. This is done in conjunction with any revision of electoral areas. The Local Election Regulation 1995 provides that in an election to a corporation of a county borough or any corporation, the first and every successive candidate elected in each electoral area shall be an alderman. So, for example, if the minister orders that there shall be two aldermen for each electoral area, the first two elected are aldermen.

Eligibility to vote in local elections

Voting in local election is by secret ballot in accordance with the proportional representation with single transferable vote in multi-member electoral areas.

The category of persons entitled to vote in local elections is broader than those which apply to any other poll. There are no citizenship requirements, and any national of any country ordinarily resident in the local electoral area, who is over 18 and is on the register is entitled to vote.[5] Electors

---

4. For a consideration of the criteria and procedure for determining local electoral areas, see Chapter 1 on Constituencies and Electoral Boundaries.
5. See Chapter 2 on Franchise and the Register of Electors.

who live in urban areas administered by borough corporations, urban district councils and town commissioners are entitled to vote at elections for both the county council and the urban authority concerned. Historical requirements that one be a ratepayer have long since been removed.

Eligibility for election to local authorities

Every person who is a citizen of Ireland or ordinarily resident in the State, who has reached the age of 18 years and is not subject to any disqualification laid down in law is eligible for election (or co-option) as a member of a local authority.

The disqualifications are set out in the Local Government Act 1994.[6] According to the Act, the following persons are ineligible for election (or co-option) as a member of a local authority:

- a member of the Commission of the European Union or a member of the European Parliament;

- a judge, advocate general or Registrar of the Court of Justice of the European Communities;

- a member of the Court of Auditors of the European Communities;

- the Ceann Comhairle of the Dáil or the Cathaoirleach of the Seanad.

- a judge appointed under the Constitution or the Comptroller and auditor general;

- a member of the Garda Síochána or a whole-time member of the defence forces;

- a civil servant who is not by terms of employment expressly permitted to be a member of a local authority;

- a person undergoing a sentence of imprisonment for any term exceeding six months;

- a person who fails to pay any portion of a sum charged or surcharged by an auditor of the accounts of any local authority, upon or

---

6.   Sections 5 and 6, Local Government Act 1994.

against that person. This disqualification has effect for a period of five years;

- a person who fails to comply with a final judgment, order or decree of a court of competent jurisdiction for payment of money due to a local authority. This disqualification applies for a period of five years;

- a person convicted of an offence relating to fraudulent or dishonest dealings affecting a local authority, corrupt practices or acting when disqualified. This disqualification lasts for five years from the closing date for appeal or one month after the order is affirmed on appeal.

The section also provided that chairpersons of certain Oireachtas committees would be disqualified from membership of local authorities. This was repealed by section 24 of the Local Government (Disclosure of Donations and Expenditure) Act 1999. It is proposed to prohibit all Oireachtas members from being members of local authorities at some stage in the future. Oireachtas members are already excluded from holding certain local authority positions, including county council chairmanships and mayoralties.

Candidates standing in more than one electoral area

One candidate can stand for election to more than one local authority, even if the elections are held on the same day. Indeed, a candidate can stand in more than one electoral area for the same local authority. However, the candidate must be nominated separately in each instance and pay separate deposits.

Where a person is elected as a member of the same local authority for two or more local electoral areas he must, within three days after the return of persons elected to be members of the local authority, write to the clerk or secretary of the relevant authority declaring which area he chooses to represent. If the newly elected member does not furnish such a written declaration they will be deemed to have chosen to represent the electoral area in which they received the greatest number of first preferences. This choice having been made the person is deemed not to have been elected for the other electoral areas and the consequential vacancies are filled in the same way as casual vacancies.

Organisation of the poll and count

The clerk or secretary of a local authority is the returning officer for the election of members to that local authority and has overall responsibility for the conduct of the poll and the count. The returning officer makes the detailed arrangements for the poll and count, which are generally the same as those set out in other chapters as applying to Dáil elections.

Nomination of candidates

The nomination procedure is in general the same as that which applies for Dáil elections. The returning officer is required not later than 28 days before polling day to give public notice of the election. Nominations must open at 10 am on the next day after the latest day on which that notice can be published and must close at 12 noon on the seventh day (disregarding an 'excluded day', i.e. a Sunday or bank holiday) following that. Candidates can nominate themselves or be nominated with their consent by an elector registered in that local electoral area.

Candidate deposits

Candidates pay a deposit, which is set by ministerial order. The Local Election Regulation 1995 sets the deposits at £50 per candidate per electoral area in respect of elections to county councils and corporations of county boroughs and at £25 for other councils.

A separate deposit must be paid in respect of each local electoral area in which the candidate is standing. However, when a candidate stands for the same council in more than one electoral area only one deposit is refunded to them, irrespective of what vote they receive.

The filling of casual vacancies on local authorities

There is no provision for by-elections to fill vacancies that arise in the membership of local authorities. The 1994 Act provides that casual vacancies are filled by the co-option by the local authority of a person to fill the vacancy. In order to qualify for co-option, a person must be qualified for membership of the local authority.

A co-option can be effected by vote if required. There is a practice in many local authorities of allowing the party of the member whose death or resignation gave rise to the vacancy to nominate the replacement candidate without a vote. However, this is merely a political practice. It has no legal basis and applies in only some local authorities.

The co-option must be made at the next meeting of the local authority after a period of fourteen days has elapsed since the vacancy occurred or as soon after that as circumstances permit. Members must be given at least three full days notice of the co-option. Where the previous holder of the vacant seat was elected as an alderman, the newly co-opted councillor does not become an alderman. The number of aldermen positions on the local authority is reduced by one until the next local election.

11 Electoral Offences, Penalties and Powers of Arrest

Personation
The offence of personation can be committed in two ways. It can occur where a person applies for a ballot paper in the name of some other person or, where a person applies for a ballot paper in their own name having already obtained a ballot paper at that election.

It is not necessary for the offender to have actually voted in somebody else's name or to have voted twice; the offence is committed merely by applying for the ballot paper. It is an offence to aid, abet, counsel or procure the commission of personation. It is also an offence for a person to vote if they are on the register but not entitled to vote, or to vote where they are not on the register at all.[1]

Bribery
Section 135 of the Electoral Act 1992 makes it an offence to procure a voter's vote for valuable consideration, or to procure the election of any person in any way for valuable consideration. In such circumstances, both the briber and the person who agrees or contracts to vote in a certain way commit offences.

It is also an offence to induce somebody to withdraw, or not to withdraw, as a candidate in return for valuable consideration. It is an offence for a person to withdraw or stay in an electoral race in consequence of such consideration. It follows, therefore, that if a candidate is bribed to withdraw, both the briber and the candidate are guilty of an offence. Aiding, abetting, counselling or procuring the commission of electoral bribery in any of these ways is also an offence.[2]

Undue influence
It is an offence to use any force, violence or restraint, to threaten or inflict an injury, or by fraud, abduction or duress to seek to induce or compel an individual:

---

1. See section 134, Electoral Act 1992.
2. See section 135, Electoral Act 1992.

- to vote or refrain from voting or vote for a certain candidate;

- to prevent an individual from freely exercising his right vote as an elector;

- to withdraw or refuse to withdraw as a candidate, to be a candidate or refrain from being a candidate, or to impede another from being a candidate.[3]

Breach of secrecy

The electoral acts give protection to the constitutional right to the secrecy of the ballot by making it an offence for any person:

- attending at the issue or opening of postal ballots, or at the counting of voting papers to attempt to ascertain the number on the back of any ballot paper;

- attending at a polling station to unlawfully communicate to another person any information as to the name or the register of elector number of any voter who has not yet applied to vote;

- to interfere or attempt to interfere with a voter when he is marking his ballot paper;

- to obtain or attempt to obtain, in a polling station, information as to how a voter is about to vote or has voted;

- to communicate to any other person any information obtained at a polling station as to who a voter has voted for;

- to directly or indirectly induce any voter to display his ballot paper after the vote has voted or to otherwise make known how he has voted;

- to interfere with or attempt to interfere with the receipt marking the return of a postal vote, or to breach the secrecy of a postal vote.[4]

Interfering with ballot boxes and ballot papers

In order to assist the smooth operation of the poll and the count and to pre-

---

3.   See section 136, Electoral Act 1992.
4.   See, for example, section 137, Electoral Act 1992.

vent any obstruction of or interference with the poll or result, the electoral legislation makes it an offence:

- to unlawfully take, destroy, conceal, open or interfere with a ballot box, or packet of ballot papers or other documents intended to be used in an election;

- to maliciously destroy, tear or deface a ballot paper;

- to forge or counterfeit a ballot paper or the official mark on a ballot paper;

- to unlawfully supply a ballot paper (or postal ballot paper) to any person;

- to fraudulently put into a ballot box any paper other than the ballot paper which one is authorised by law to put in it;

- to unlawfully take a ballot paper out of a polling station;

- to unlawfully mark a ballot paper while acting or purporting to act as a companion to an illiterate, blind or incapacitated voter.

- to forge or fraudulently deface any official envelope or form of declaration identity or form of receipt used in connection with special voting or postal voting, or any other formal document used at an election;

Interference with nomination process
It is an offence:

- to forge or fraudulently deface or destroy any nomination paper or any certificate of political affiliation or any authorisations under section 99 or section 100 of the 1992 Act.

- to produce to the returning officer a nomination paper one knows to be forged;

- to produce to the returning officer a certificate of party affiliation which one knows to be forged;[5]

---

5. See section 142, Electoral Act 1992.

- to nominate or withdraw a person's candidature without their consent;[6]

- to knowingly publish a false statement that a candidate has withdrawn or died;

- to violently obstruct the nomination of candidates;[7]

- to make a false declaration (whether as a candidate or a proposer) that one believes the candidate to be eligible for election when one does not have reasonable grounds for so believing and when the candidate is not eligible to stand as a candidate.[8]

Interference with the official mark
It is an offence:

- to counterfeit the official mark;

- to unlawfully remove, destroy or damage the instruments for making the official mark, or to make or to have in one's possession any imitation or counterfeit of any such instrument;

- for any person attending at the issue of postal ballot papers or attending at a polling station to communicate any information about the official mark to any other person before the close of the poll.

Campaigning in the vicinity of a polling station
A person can be prosecuted for obstruction and interference with electors if he interferes with, obstructs or impedes an elector going to or coming from or in the vicinity of a polling station.

Furthermore, one commits an offence if, on polling day – during the period beginning 30 minutes before the opening of the poll and finishing 30 minutes after the closing of the poll – within the curtilage of a polling station or anywhere within 100 metres of a polling station one:

- loiters or congregates with other persons.

- canvasses (induces, by any means whatsoever, an elector to vote for

---

6.   See section 141, Electoral Act 1992.
7.   See section 145, Electoral Act 1992.
8.   See section 143, Electoral Act 1992.

a candidate or candidates or vote in a particular way or refrain from voting);

- displays or distributes any notice or sign or poster or card or circular or other document relating to the election (except returning officer posters and notices);

- uses or causes to be used any loud speaker or other public address mechanism to broadcast matter relating to the election.

The 100 metre distance is measured from any entrance to the polling station or the grounds of the polling station.

Political activity by polling staff
It is an offence for a returning officer, an assistant deputy or acting returning officer or any person employed by any returning officer for the purpose of the election to act as agent for or be actively associated in furthering the candidature of any candidate or promoting the interests of any political party.

Penalties for the above offences
A person found guilty of any the above offences is liable;

- on summary conviction to a fine not exceeding £1,000 or, at the discretion of the court, to a period of imprisonment not exceeding six months, or both; and

- on conviction on indictment to a fine not exceeding £2,500 or, at the discretion of the court, to a period of imprisonment not exceeding two years, or both.

Minor electoral offences and penalties
A person found guilty of committing one of the following offences is liable on summary conviction to a fine not exceeding £500 and/or up to three months imprisonment.

Registration offences
- Knowingly furnishing false information in a claim for correction of the draft register;

- Failing to give information, or knowingly giving false information when further information is required by a registering authority;

- Making a statement pursuant to section 12 of the Electoral Act 1997 in the name of another person;

- Applying to be registered on the special register in the name of another person.

The Act also makes it an offence to unlawfully destroy or damage any draft register, notice, copy of the register of electors, election list or other documents made available for public inspection in connection with the preparation of the register. These offences may be prosecuted by the local authority itself.

Failing to give printer and publisher details on election literature
It is an offence to print, publish or post, or cause to be printed, published or posted, any election literature (every bill, poster or similar document having reference to an election or distributed for the purpose of furthering the candidature of any candidate at an election) which does not bear upon its face the name and address of the printer and publisher thereof.[9]
    Material printed by the returning officer is exempt from this requirement. Printing is defined as including "the producing of copies by any process, other than by hand".

Personation agent leaving polling station without permission
A personation agent commits an offence if he leaves a polling station without the permission of the presiding officer and without first leaving all registers, books and documents in which he has made any notes, with the presiding officer.

Handling ballot papers at the count
It is an offence for a candidate or the agent of a candidate to handle a ballot paper during the counting of the votes.

Powers of arrest
A presiding officer can request a garda to remove any person who misconducts himself at a polling station or fails to obey the orders of the presiding officers.
    Where a presiding officer at a polling station has reasonable cause to believe that a person who is applying or has applied for a ballot is committing or has committed personation, he may direct a member of the Garda Síochána to arrest the person before leaving the polling station.

---

9.   See section 140, Electoral Act 1992.

Where a presentation agent for one of the candidates at a polling station declares, and undertakes in writing to prove, that an elector has committed personation, the presiding officer can similarly request such an arrest. Again, this must take place before the elector leaves the polling station.

A garda who has reasonable cause to believe that a person is committing or has committed personation can arrest such a person on his own motion. This Garda power extends to making the arrest anywhere.

Compensation for unproven allegation of personation

The Act encourages personation agents to proceed cautiously when asking the presiding officer to exercise his power to ask a garda to arrest a voter on suspicion of personation.

Where a person is arrested, and either the personation agent (or someone on his behalf) fails to appear before the court to support the charge or the court acquits the person and finds that the charge was made by the personation agent without reasonable or just cause, the court may, at the request of the person charged and not otherwise, order the personation agent to pay an amount of up to £500 by way of damages. This payment is deemed to be full satisfaction of any claim for damages on the part of the accused person arising from being charged, arrested or detained, i.e. if he goes this route, he has no other civil remedy against the personation agent who, without just cause, accuses him of personation.[10]

---

10. See section 158, Electoral Act 1992.

12 A Note on the Public Offices Commission

The Public Offices Commission was established on 1 November 1995. The legal basis of its establishment and membership are to be found in Ethics in Public Office Act 1995. The commission plays a number of roles, mainly in supervising and assisting in the implementation of the various systems of controls and regulation imposed on candidates, Oireachtas members, officeholders and public servants under the Ethics in Public Office Act 1995 and the Electoral Act 1997, as amended by the Electoral Act 1998.

The detailed role of the commission in each of these areas is outlined in the following chapters. However, it is instructive at this point to outline the commission's membership and to give an overview of its role.

Membership

The commission membership is specified in the 1995 Act, and includes:

- the Comptroller and Auditor General;

- the Ombudsman;

- the Chairman of the Dáil;

- the Clerk of the Dáil;

- the Clerk of the Seanad.

The commission itself appoints one of its members to be chairperson of the commission and that person holds office for as long as is determined by the commission itself. If the chairperson ceases to be a member of the commission, he also ceases to be chairperson, and a new chairperson is elected. The members of the commission are independent in the performance of their function under the acts. The secretariat of the commission is provided by the office of the Ombudsman on a secondment basis.

Functions of the Public Offices Commission

The role of the Public Offices Commission is to publish guidelines, to provide advice and to assist in compliance with the Ethics in Public Office Act 1995 and to investigate and report in relation to possible contraventions of the Act. The commission also has the principal supervisory role under the Electoral Act 1997 dealing with the disclosure of political donations, public funding of political parties, the capping of election expenses and the recoupment of certain electoral expenses.

It should be noted that, as will become clear in the following chapters, the commission is not always the body or, in some instances, the only body involved in assisting and enforcing compliance with the acts. For example, it is significant that the Committee on Members Interests, which has the primary role in relation to the ethics obligations of members in both the Dáil and Seanad and the system of election expenditure and donations statements for local elections, was established outside the ambit of the Public Offices Commission.

Guidelines and advice

The commission has a statutory obligation to produce guidelines and advice on what is required by public representatives, officeholders and public servants in relation to the operation of the Acts. In addition, under the Acts, the commission may on request provide advice in relation to the provisions of the Acts in a particular case.

The commission, after consultation with the relevant Committee on Members Interests, is required to draw up and publish guidelines for officeholders and public servants covered by the Ethics in Public Office Act 1995. It also publishes detailed guidelines for candidates and agents in respect of the various elections that come within its remit.

The commission can give advice on request to a person covered by the Act on the meaning or application of any provision of the 1995 Act. The commission must respond within 21 days with the advice or with notification that the advice will be provided. The persons covered by the Act are obliged to act in accordance with the advice given and the guidelines published by the commission unless by so doing they would be contravening another provision of the act.

Ensuring compliance and undertaking investigations

The commission has statutory powers to undertake enquiries into breaches under the Acts. Where appropriate it can refer the results of such an investigation to the Director of Public Prosecutions for possible prosecution.

Public access to statements
The commission is required to provide access to the public to examine or photocopy all statements of donations and election expenses and some of the declarations of interest required under the Acts.

13 Election Expenditure Controls and Disclosures

Legislative framework

The Electoral Act 1997 lays down a complex mechanism for the control and limiting of election expenditure by political parties and candidates which can be applied to Dáil, European and presidential elections. In light of the experiences of candidates and parties endeavouring to comply with the controls during the 1997 presidential election and during by-elections, amending legislation was enacted in 1998 to clarify and alter the controls and limits detailed in the 1997 Act.

The 1997 Act also enabled the Minister for the Environment to introduce regulations to control expenditure in local elections. This provision was never used and, in advance of the 1999 local elections, the Local Elections (Disclosure of Donations and Expenditure) Act 1999 was passed. This Act now governs expenditure controls in respect of local authority polls.

In order to limit election expenditure, it was necessary to establish an elaborate system to monitor, account for and record election expenditure. This involves requiring political parties and candidates to appoint agents and to account for their election expenditure. The Acts listed above also impose restrictions on how and when services and facilities provided to political parties and candidates during elections can be ordered and paid for.

What constitutes an election expense?

'Election expenditure' is defined in the Acts as all expenditure incurred in connection with an election in order to promote or oppose, directly or indirectly, the interests of a political party, to present the policies or particular policies of a political party or the comments of a political party or of one or more candidates, to solicit votes for or against a party or otherwise to influence the outcome of an election.[1] The definition of 'election expenses' in the Acts expressly includes any expenditure by or on behalf of a party or a candidate on the undertaking of opinion polls or similar surveys within 60 days before polling day.

---

1. Section 31, Electoral Act 1997 and section 6, Local Elections (Disclosure of Donations and Expenditure) Act 1999.

Where property, goods or services are provided free or at a reduced rate to candidates or political parties, they are deemed to be an election expense and to have been provided at a commercial rate and must be included as such in the relevant statements of election expenses. It follows that if a printer prints 10,000 canvass cards for a candidate and charges him £8,000 where the commercial rate for this printing would be £10,000, it is accounted as £10,000 of electoral expenses on behalf of the candidate.

All election expenses incurred by a person or body associated with the candidate or political party are deemed to be expenditure on the part of the candidate or party and therefore must be declared in the relevant election expenditure statement.

The 'election period'

In an important adjustment to the original definition of election expenses, the 1998 Act provides that the term 'election expenses' incorporates only election expenditure on goods, property or services for use during the election period.[2]

The relevant 'election period' is defined by as follows:

- in respect of Dáil elections, the election period commences on the date of the dissolution of the Dáil and ends on polling day;

- in respect of all presidential, local[3] and European elections and Dáil by-elections, the election period commences on the date on which the ministerial order setting the polling day is made and finishes on the date of polling day.

It should be noted, however, that election expenditure incurred before the election period on goods, services or property for use during the election period is also regarded as an election expense, which falls within the limit and must be accounted for in the election expenditure statement.

What expenditure is excluded from the definition of election expenses?

The Acts specifically provide that certain expenditure is deemed not to constitute election expenditure and does not therefore fall within the ambit of these controls and limits. The types of exempted expenditure are:

- the payment of a deposit required for candidate nomination;

---

2. See section 10, Electoral (Amendment) Act 1998.
3. See section 3, Local Elections (Disclosure of Donations and Expenditure) Act 1999.

- payments for any copies of the register of elector;

- what the Acts call "the reasonable living expenses" of a candidate or of any person working on behalf of the candidate on a voluntary basis;

- any minor, 'out of pocket' expenses lawfully incurred by any person in relation to the election if those out of pocket expenses are not reimbursed;

- free postage facilities provided to candidates in certain elections;

- party political broadcasts provided to candidates and parties by law. It should be noted that whereas the provision of the broadcast time is not regarded as reckonable election expenditure, the cost of making the party political broadcast, whether sound recording costs or video production costs, is deemed to be an election expense;

- facilities, services or payments provided to Oireachtas or European Parliament members by European Union or other intergovernmental organisations by reason of their office;

- expenditure incurred in the provision of property, goods or services that were provided for a previous election and already included on an election expenses statement in that election. For example, if a candidate uses the same posters as he used in the previous election, the print costs of those posters, which would have been declared in the last election, would not have to be declared in this election.

The 1998 Act specifically exempted two further items:

- assistance or services provided by an employee of a political party, provided they are not in receipt of extra remuneration;

- a service rendered by a person, including the use of that person's motor vehicle, where it is provided free *gratis* and is not part of that individual's employment, business or profession. For example, where a party supporter provides his car to ferry voters to the poll on polling day, it would not be deemed an election expense. However, if a taxi driver were to do so, it would amount to an election expense.

Appointment of party national agents in elections

Each party is required by law to appoint a 'national agent' for the purpose of accounting for and controlling election expenditure in Dáil, European and local elections. The party must notify the Public Offices Commission (or local authority) of the identity and address of the national agent, not later than the last day for the close of nominations. If the party does not notify the Public Offices Commission by that date the 'appropriate officer' appointed for the donation and payment provisions of the Electoral Act 1997 is deemed to be the national agent for the expenditure provisions. The names of the national agents must be published in *Iris Oifigiúil.*

The national agent must make all contracts entered into by the party, which involve the spending of money for election purposes. No election expense shall be incurred by the party and no payment or deposit can be made in respect of an election expense other than by the national agent or with his expressed authority.

The incurring of an election expense by any subsidiary body of the party, branch member or any body which "a reasonable person would believe [is] controlled or substantially influenced by" that political party or candidate is deemed to be election expenditure incurred by the party or candidate.

Where a political party has a candidate or several candidates standing in both Dáil and European elections held on the same day, the party must appoint the same person as national agent for both elections and make a single combined statement of election expenditure to the Public Offices Commission.

Appointment of candidate election agents in Dáil and European elections

Each candidate in a Dáil or European election is required to appoint an election agent for the purpose of these Acts. The appointment must be notified to the constituency returning officer who arranges for the publication of the names of the election agents.

A candidate can appoint himself as election agent and, if a named individual is not appointed election agent before the close of nominations, the returning officer is to assume that the candidate has appointed himself as the election agent.

The appointment of a national or election agent can be revoked at any time. Where a vacancy occurs in this way or otherwise, another agent must be appointed forthwith.

All contracts, which involve the incurring of election expense by the candidate, must be made by the election agent. No election expense can be incurred on behalf of the candidate and no payment or deposit on an election expense can be made other than by the election agent or with his express authority. The election agent must be given details and vouchers of any election expenditure incurred on behalf of the candidate before the election agent was appointed.

A candidate who is a candidate in both a Dáil and European election, which take place on the same day, must appoint the same person as agent for both the Dáil and European elections and make a single combined election expense statement to the Public Offices Commission.

Election expenditure by 'third parties'

A third party for the purpose of the Acts is a party (i.e. person, company or body) who is not connected to a political party or candidate. The Acts require that where a person, other than the national agent, election agent, candidate or person authorised by them, intends to incur election expenditure (i.e. to spend money in support of a particular party, candidate or policy) they must first notify the Public Offices Commission. The notification must include details of the nature and purpose and estimated amount of the expenditure, the details of the person purporting to incur the expenditure and details of the connection, if any, which the person or body has with any candidate or party.

Within five days after polling day, a body or person who incurs this type of expenditure must furnish an election expenses statement to the Public Offices Commission (or the local authority). If a body or person fails to make this return, they are liable, on summary conviction, to a fine of up to £1,000. If a person or body makes a statement to the commission, which they know to be false or inaccurate, they are liable, on conviction on indictment, to a fine of to £20,000 and a prison sentence of up to three years.

Controls on the ordering of and payment for electoral goods and services by candidates and parties

The Acts lay down the following control mechanisms, which must be complied with, not only by the parties and candidates but also by those providing goods or services to them for the purpose of the election.

- Every payment of election expenses above a certain figure (£500) must be supported by a voucher stating the particulars of the transaction to which it relates (i.e. an invoice).

- The publisher of a newspaper or magazine, etc. cannot publish any advertisement for or against a candidate or party or their policies unless the booking of the advertisement is made by the national agent or an election agent, a candidate or some person authorised in writing by them. Where the advertisement is booked by a body or person other than a candidate or agent (i.e. a 'third party'), that person must produce a certificate from the Public Offices Commission (or local authority) that they have complied with the notification requirement to the Commission as outlined above.

- Every claim in respect of election expenses against the national agent of a political party, a candidate's election agent or a candidate must be delivered to the agent before the 45th day after the poll. Any claim presented after that date is not enforceable. If a claim which relates to election expenses is not delivered within that 45-day period, it must not be paid and is not enforceable against the agent or person in question.

Allocation of the expenditure limit between candidates and parties

Where a candidate represents a political party, the party can incur a portion of the expenditure that the candidate is entitled to incur. The candidate must consent in a written agreement to assign a portion of his limit over to the party. This agreement must be submitted to the Public Offices Commission with the election expenditure statements. The portion of his limit that the candidate could sign over to the party nationally had been limited to 50 per cent by the 1997 Act, but this limit was removed by the 1998 amending Act and no such restriction currently applies.

Expenditure by a political party in a Dáil or European constituency, other than expenditure by the national agent of the party, is deemed to be expenditure incurred by the candidate and must be accounted for by the election agent of the candidate.

The election expenditure limit on a party's national campaign is calculated by totalling the portions of their limits, which have been assigned in writing by each candidate to the party nationally.

If a Dáil and European election are held on the same day, and a person is standing in both elections, the limit on their expenditure is the figure for the European constituency in which they are standing plus three-quarters of the figure for the Dáil constituency in which they are also standing.

Election expenditure limits

Dáil Élections

The aggregate election expenses of candidates in Dáil elections set down by the 1997 Act are as follows:

- £14,000 per candidate in a three-seat constituency;

- £17,000 per candidate in a four-seat constituency;

- £20,000 per candidate in a five-seat constituency.

European elections
The 1997 Act did not specify the limits applicable to European elections, but provided that they could be fixed by ministerial order. The order in respect of the 1999 European election set the limit of election expenditure that may be incurred by, or on behalf of, each candidate at £150,000. The limit is the same irrespective of the number of members to be elected for each constituency.

Presidential elections
The limit on expenditure for presidential elections is not specified in the Act but again is laid down by a ministerial order in the lead up to each presidential election. The Act requires that the Minister, in fixing the limits, should have regard to the limit set down for Dáil and European elections and to the rate of inflation. The ministerial regulation in respect of the presidential election of November 1997 did not set an expenditure limit.

Local elections
The Local Elections (Disclosure of Donations and Expenditure) Act 1999 provided that there should be no limit on candidate expenditure in respect of local elections, which in fact repealed that section of the 1997 Act that had empowered the Minister to impose such a limit.

Expenditure statements and controls in Dáil and European elections

Each political party's national agent must, within 56 days after polling day, furnish a detailed statement to the Public Offices Commission of all election expenses incurred by the party, accompanied by vouchers for these expenses. The national agent must also furnish details of each candidate authenticated by the party in the election and details of all agreements in writing between the party and each candidate, assigning portions of expenditure limits to the party as described above.

Each candidate's election agent must, within 56 days of polling day, also furnish a detailed statement to the Public Offices Commission of the election expenses incurred – whether paid or not – on the candidate's behalf in respect of the election. The election agent of a party candidate must also include details of any agreement between the candidate and the party allotting a portion of the candidate's spending limit to the party.

Both statements must be accompanied by a statutory declaration. An obligation is imposed on national agents and election agents to maintain records and make such enquiries as are necessary to make the statement. These statements are published by laying them before both Houses of the Oireachtas and are available for inspection and copying at the offices of the Public Offices Commission.

Expenditure statements and controls in presidential elections

In the main, the provisions regarding presidential election agents are the same as those for Dáil and European elections with the following key distinctions.

In a presidential election, parties are not required to appoint national party agents. Instead a presidential election agent is appointed by each candidate and all expenditure incurred by all political parties supporting that candidate is deemed to be expenditure on behalf of the candidate, and the candidate's agent must account for it.[4]

Each presidential election candidate must notify the presidential returning officer of the appointment of an election agent, not later than the last day for the close of nominations. The candidate can appoint herself as the election agent, and indeed if the returning officer has not been notified of an appointment before the close of nominations, it is assumed that the candidate is also to be the agent. The presidential returning officer notifies the Public Offices Commission of the appointment of each presidential election agent.

As is the case with other elections, all contracts must be made by the presidential election agent or on his express authority and all election expenditure must be incurred and paid for by the election agent. In the case of presidential elections, all expenses above £500 must be vouched for.

Within 56 days after polling day, each candidate's presidential election agent must furnish a statement of election expenses to the Public Offices Commission. Election expenses are defined similarly to those for Dáil and European elections as outlined and the statement is in a similar form. Details of the expenses and copies of the vouchers for all items, which involve expenditure above £500, must be provided. As mentioned above, all election expenditure of any party supporting the presidential election candidate is deemed to be expenditure on behalf of the candidate and the details of such expenditure must be included in the presidential election agent's expenses. As with the expenditure statements in the Dáil and European elections, the presidential election expenditure statements are

---

4.   For example, in the 1997 presidential election, expenditure by Fianna Fáil and the Progressive Democrats was accounted for by Mary McAleese's election agent, as her candidature was supported by both parties, similarly, expenditure by the Labour Party, the Green Party, and Democratic Left was accounted for by Adi Roche's election agent.

published and are available for inspection and copying at the offices of the Public Offices Commission.

Similar requirements to those that apply in other elections are imposed on persons or bodies wishing to incur election expenditure in support of a presidential election candidate. They must notify the Public Offices Commission in advance and make a statement of election expenses after the election. The restrictions on newspapers and magazines accepting advertising in support of a presidential candidate also operate in the manner outlined above.

Expenditure statements and controls in local elections

As outlined above, although the 1997 Act provided that its provisions regarding controls and limits on election expenditure could be extended by ministerial order to local elections, the government decided in advance of the local elections in June 1999 to introduce new legislation to cover local elections.

The Local Elections (Disclosure of Donations and Expenditure) Act 1999 provides for a system of controls and statements relating to election expenditure. It differs in a number of significant respects with the system operating for other elections.

First, there are no limits on the election expenditure which parties or candidates can incur.

Second, the system to control expenditure was established outside the remit of the Public Offices Commission. The system is operated and policed by the relevant local authority and statements are made to the relevant secretary or clerk. Parties are required to appoint national agents for the local elections to account for and control expenditure at national level. The national agent for local elections has 90 days in which to make the expenditure statements. These statements are not made to the Public Offices Commission but rather to a designated local authority. Dublin Corporation was the designated authority for the purposes of the 1999 local elections.

Third, in addition to the national agent, the party is required to appoint a 'designated person' in each local electoral area in which it has candidates standing. This person, who could be described as a "local area party agent", is required to submit a statement to the relevant local authority detailing all election expenditure by the party in respect of the election in that local electoral area.

Fourth, there is no requirement in local elections that candidates appoint election agents. The candidates themselves make the required declarations and returns. Any contract under which election expenses exceeding £500 in value are incurred must be made by the candidate.

The election expenditure statement, detailing all election expenses, must be made by each candidate not later than 90 days after the poll. In addition to declaring the expenditure, the candidate must state how the expenses were met as well as providing details of any donation received by the candidate, which exceeded £500 in value.[5]

The election expenditure and donation statement is made to the secretary or clerk of the local authority to which the candidate is seeking election. Once submitted, these forms are available for public inspection at the relevant council offices.

Fifth, it is the local authority rather than the Public Offices Commission that investigates any complaints about the election expense statements and ultimately, on the advice of the DPP, prosecutes any offences which arise, including failure to file a statement or filing a false statement.

Third-party election expenditure declarations, as outlined above, are also made to the local authority.

Absence of controls and limits in Seanad elections
Interestingly, the Electoral Act 1997 made no provision for any expenditure controls or limits in Seanad elections, which can prove at least as expensive for candidates as Dáil elections.

Minor errors in election expenditure statements
The Acts provide that if an election (or donation) statement contains a minor error or omission, the Public Offices Commission (or local authority) shall furnish details of the error to the candidate who has fourteen days in which to correct it. A copy of the amended statement is made public in the same way as the original statement.

Offences and penalties

Breach of limits and controls
The party's national agent, a candidate's election agent, or candidate in a Dáil, European or presidential election commits an offence if he knowingly:

* incurs an election expense above the limit where there is one;

* pays any election expense not claimed within 45 days of the poll;

* fails to furnish the required election expenses statement in the required detail and form by the relevant deadline.

5.   See section 10, Local Elections (Disclosure of Donations and Expenditure) Act 1999.

In each of these instances, summary conviction renders an individual liable to a fine of up to £1,000.

Financial penalties on parties
Where a party, or its candidates, exceeds the expenditure limit in an election, calculated as outlined above, the Minister for Finance must, when so advised by the Public Offices Commission, deduct the amount by which the party has exceeded the limit from the Exchequer payments to the party in the year following that election.[6]

Financial penalties on candidates
Where a candidate or his agent exceeds the limit imposed on his level of election expenditure, the Minister for Finance, when so advised by the Public Offices Commission or relevant local authority, must deduct the amount by which the limit has been exceeded from the reimbursement of election expenses paid to that candidate.

False or misleading expenditure statements
Where an agent in a Dáil, European or presidential election furnishes an election expenses statement, which the agent knows to be false or misleading in a material respect, the agent, on conviction on indictment, is liable to a fine of up to £20,000 and a prison sentence of up to three years.

Exclusion from Oireachtas or European Parliament membership
There is no provision in the 1997 or 1998 Electoral Acts for the removal of a TD, MEP or president for a breach of the provisions of the Acts. Such a provision in respect of a president would be unconstitutional. However, breaches of expenditure limits and controls can be a factor which courts may consider in electoral petitions.

Exclusion from membership of a local authority
The Local Elections (Disclosure of Donations and Expenditure) Act 1999 provides that, where an unsuccessful candidate at a local election fails to furnish an election expenditure statement and accompanying statutory declaration within the 90-day period, he is liable to disqualification from membership of a local authority (including co-option) until the next local elections.[7]

The 1999 Act also provides that where a successful member fails to furnish an election expenditure statement within 90 days then he is suspended from membership of the local authority for seven days or lesser period

---

6. Such a fine was imposed on Fine Gael for breaching the expenditure limit in the 1998 Limerick East by-election. See the Public Offices Commission's annual report 1998.
7. See section 20, 1999 Act.

until the statement and statutory declaration are provided. If they are still not provided within the seven days then the elected member will be disqualified from membership of a local authority (including co-option) until the next local election.

If an elected or unelected member furnishes a statement or statutory declaration, which to the member's knowledge is false or misleading in a material respect, they may be prosecuted by the local authority under the Statutory Declarations Act 1938. If convicted, they will be disqualified from membership of a local authority until the next local elections.

Wrongful publication of an election advertisement

The Acts provide that a publisher of a newspaper, magazine or other publication is guilty of an offence if he publishes an advertisement or notice purporting to promote the interest of a party or candidate at the request of any person other than a candidate or agent or a person authorised in writing by them unless that person has certificate from the Public Offices Commission (or local authority).[8]

Inadvertent error or omission

In what could be called a 'benefit of the doubt' provision, the Electoral Act 1997 specifically provides that, where a prosecution is made for one of these offences under the Acts and the failure, error, omission or misleading statement occurred due to the illness, death, absence or misconduct of a party or candidate's agent, or was due to inadvertence or other reasonable cause, not involving negligence, and there was no lack of bona fides on the part of the agent, or where the offence was due to the misconduct of any other person of which the agent did not approve or was not aware, the court can take this into account and grant such relief as it thinks fit.

It is a defence, where an agent is accused of breach of the election expenditure limit for the agent, to show that he did not know or could not know that the election expense, which was above the limit, was incurred. Furthermore, where an agent commits a breach of the controls or limits and the party or candidate was not aware that the agent had committed the breach and took all reasonable action to prevent the breach, the court can have regard to this and not punish the party.

---

8.   See section 43 Electoral Act 1997 and section 21, Local Election Act 1999.

14 Exchequer Funding of Political Parties and Reimbursement of Candidates' Expenses

Exchequer funding of political parties

The largest amount of public funding provided to political parties by the Exchequer is allocated under the provisions of Part III of the Electoral Act 1997. The Act establishes a process whereby the State makes an annual payment to 'qualified political parties' for non-election related administration, research and organisation expenses. There are strict terms and conditions with which the parties must comply in order to receive the funding.

Qualified political parties

A 'qualified political party' is a party that is registered in the Register of Political Parties as a party organised in the State to contest a Dáil election and which secured not less than 2 per cent of the national first preference vote in the previous general election.[1]

Allocation of funding between parties

The legislation capped the total annual payment to all qualified political parties at £1 million per annum.[2] However, provision is made in the legislation for an increase in this total in line with general increases in civil service pay. Accordingly, when the first annual payments came to be made in 1998, the total fund was £1,030,347.[3]

The amount must be divided between the parties in accordance with their percentage share of the national first preference poll in the preceding general election. A party's national first preference total is ascertained by totalling the first preference vote received by all of that party's candidates in all constituencies and expressing it as a percentage of the total national valid poll. The payments are made in quarterly instalments to party headquarters by the Minister for Finance after the Public Offices Commission certifies that the party has complied with the terms and conditions set out in the Act.

In a year in which a general election is held, payment up to polling day is

---

1. Section 16, Electoral Act 1997.
2. Section 17, Electoral Act 1997.
3. See the Public Offices Commission's Annual Report 1998, page 45.

calculated with reference to the first preference vote in the previous election. The outstanding payment for the portion of the year falling after polling day is calculated with reference to the result of the new general election.

Restrictions on the uses to which Exchequer funding can be put
There are restrictions regarding the use of this annual payment by political parties. It must be used for:

- the general administration of the party;

- research, education and training;

- policy formulation;

- co-ordination of the activities of the branches and members of the party.

The payments made to parties under the Electoral Act 1997 are deemed to include provision for the promotion of participation by women and young people in political activity.[4]

The Act specifically provides that annual payments cannot be used for expenditure incurred in Dáil, Seanad, European, presidential, local or Údarás na Gaeltachta elections.

Expenditure statement
Each political party must provide an annual audited statement certifying that the funding was used for one or all of the purposes outlined above.[5]

The statement must also indicate the matters to which the payment were actually applied, including the amounts applied to the promotion of participation by women and young persons in political activity.

The statements and the auditor's reports are laid before each House of the Oireachtas and they are held at the office of the Public Offices Commission for inspection or copying. Payment for the ensuing year must be withheld pending the submission of this audited statement and of the annual donation statement, which is also required of each party.[6]

Funding for independent members of the Dáil and the Seanad
The legislation states that the Minister for the Environment may provide,

---

4. This replaces previous Exchequer grants to political parties specifically for Youth Political Education Officers.
5. The accounts must be audited by a 'Public Auditor'; see Section 20, Electoral Act 1997.
6. See Chapter 15 on Statements of Political Donations.

by regulation, for the payment of additional financial support – over and above the secretarial assistance available to Deputies – to members of the Dáil who are not members of a qualified political party (e.g. independents) to assist them in the discharge of their parliamentary functions.

Reimbursement of expenses to candidates in Dáil elections

The Electoral Act 1997 also establishes a system of payment to qualifying Dáil candidates by way of a reimbursement of election expenses.[7] The amount which can be paid to each candidate is limited by the legislation. The current limit is the total amount of election expenditure incurred by the candidate or £5,000, whichever is the lower.[8] The money is payable to Dáil candidates in both general elections and by-elections. In order to qualify, a candidate must have achieved at least one-quarter of the quota either in first preference votes or in first preference votes and transfers.

The candidate must apply for the payment to the Public Offices Commission and the candidate's election agent must provide the Public Offices Commission with the required statement of election expenses and a supporting statutory declaration. The candidate must prove that he actually incurred the expenditure during the campaign. The 1998 Act amended the 1997 Act to specify that expenditure by a party in a constituency, including expenditure by the national agent, will be deemed to be expenditure by a candidate for the purpose of the reimbursement of the candidate's election expenses.[9]

Reimbursement of expenses to candidates in European elections

Whereas the 1997 Act actually specifies the procedure for payment to Dáil election candidates, it gives the Minister the power to introduce regulations governing the payment of similar reimbursements of election expenses to candidates in presidential and European elections. The Minister is required to place a draft of the regulation before each House of the Oireachtas and the regulation cannot be made until each House passes a resolution approving the draft.

The European Parliament Election (Reimbursement of Expenses) Regulation in respect of the 1999 European elections provided for the reimbursement of election expenses for each candidate.[10] The amount to be reimbursed was the actual expenses incurred by the candidate or £35,000, whichever is the greater. Candidates must again furnish to the Public

---

7. See section 21, Electoral Act 1997.
8. The Act provides that the Minister may vary by order the amounts and limits specified in the Act in line with changes in the consumer price index.
9. Section 5, Electoral Act 1998.
10. SI No. 122 of 1999.

Offices Commission the required statement of expenditure and vouchers, in accordance with the guidelines, before the reimbursement payment can be made by the Minister for Finance.

Reimbursement of expenses to candidates in presidential elections

The 1997 Act enables the Minister to introduce regulations to provide for the reimbursement of election expenses to presidential election candidates. However, the Presidential Election Regulation 1997 made no provision for a reimbursement of any presidential election candidate expenditure.

Absence of reimbursement of expenses to candidates in Seanad and local elections

No provision is made for the reimbursement of the election expenses of candidates in a Seanad election, although these elections can prove to be at least as expensive as Dáil elections. Similarly, no provision was made in the original 1997 Act or in the 1999 Act for the reimbursement of the election expenses of candidates in local elections.

15 Statements of Political Donations

Statements of donations by political parties

Each year, before 31 March, each political party must furnish a statement to the Public Offices Commission giving details of all donations over £4,000 that it received in the previous year. This statement must give the amount of each donation above £4,000 together with the name, address and description of the donor.

A donation to any 'subsidiary organisation' of a political party is deemed to be a donation to the political party. A 'subsidiary organisation' is defined in section 22 of the Electoral Act 1997 as including not only any associate or body that forms part of the political party or was established or has functions bestowed on it by the political party, but also any body or association, which is effectively controlled by the political party or by the officers of the political party.

Statements of donations by TDs, Senators and MEPs

Each year, before 31 January, every member of the Oireachtas and every Member of the European Parliament must furnish a statement to the Public Offices Commission giving details of any donations above £500 received in the previous year. The statement must include the amount of the donation, and the name, description and postal address of the donor.

Statements of donations by unsuccessful candidates in Dáil and European elections

Within 56 days after polling day, each unsuccessful candidate in a Dáil, Seanad or European election must furnish a statement to the Public Offices Commission giving details of any donations above £500 they received in relation to that election. These donation statements are also required of unsuccessful candidates in Dáil by-elections. Successful candidates are not required to make this declaration, but of course will have to declare such donations as part of the annual declaration required of TDs, Senators and MEPs as outlined above.

It is important to note that the 1997 Act applies to all donations in relation to the election, including donations received before the writ for the

101

Dáil election was moved or the order appointing the date for the Seanad or European election was made.

Statements of donations by candidates in presidential elections

The donation statements of presidential election candidates are made by their presidential election agents. Again, the declaration must include donations received where the value is greater than £500. The declaration must be made to the Public Offices Commission within 56 days after the poll. A statement of donations must be made by the agent of the successful candidate (i.e. the new president) as well as the agents of unsuccessful candidates. Interestingly, the president, unlike TDs, Senators or MEPs, is not required to make an annual statement of political donations received.

The statement must include the name and address of the donor and the amount of all donations above £500. This declaration must be accompanied by a statutory declaration and an obligation is imposed on the presidential election agent to make whatever enquiries and to keep whatever records are necessary to make this declaration.

Statements of donations by candidates in Seanad elections

The provisions of the Electoral Act 1997 in respect of statements of donations also apply to Seanad elections and by-elections. The relevant threshold is again £500, and the statement must be made to the Public Offices Commission within 56 days of the close of poll. However, there is no requirement for parties to make donation statements in respect of Seanad elections or for the parties of Seanad candidates to appoint agents.

Statements of donations by candidates in local elections

The Electoral Act 1997 provided for the extension of a requirement to declare election donations to local elections by ministerial order. However, in advance of the June 1999 local elections, new legislation was introduced to cover local elections. Under the terms of the Local Elections (Disclosure of Donations and Expenditure) Act 1999, local election candidates are required to declare any donation above £500. In this instance, the declaration is not made to the Public Offices Commission, but rather details of donations above £500 are part of a declaration on campaign funding and expenditure, which the candidate is required to make to the relevant local authority within 90 days of polling day.

Statements required of certain donors

The Electoral (Amendment) Act 1998 introduced a requirement that certain donors (primarily private individuals) disclose to the Public Offices

Commission donations exceeding an aggregate value of £4,000 where the donations are made to:

- two or more persons who, when the donations were made, were members of the same political party; or

- one or more persons and to the political party of which such person(s) were members when the donation were made to them.

The 1998 Act removed the requirement contained in the 1997 Act that parties themselves aggregate for disclosure purposes all donations from the same person or source which were given to the party at any level or to any of its candidates. This requirement had proved impractical and was replaced with this more workable requirement whereby the donor keeps track of such donations and is responsible for declaring them to the Public Offices Commission should the aggregate value exceed the £4,000 threshold.

If the donations from one donor source exceed the threshold, they must be declared. A donor source could be one private individual, a group of connected persons, a company or group of companies. In addition to making this declaration to the Public Offices Commission, a company must declare in their annual returns to the Companies Office, any donation the aggregate of which given to one party exceeds £4,000, thereby publishing them.

This declaration must be made irrespective of whether the individual donations are greater or less than £500 and are declarable by the individual recipient. If the total of all the donations in one year to one party is greater than the party limit of £4,000, the donor must declare it. Failure by a donor to make this donation statement is an offence. The 1998 Act reinforced this requirement by prohibiting any party member or candidate from accepting a donation from a donor if the recipient knows or has reason to believe that the donor in question will be required to make a donation statement and does not intend to do so.

If a donation is received in breach of this prohibition, the Public Offices Commission must be notified and the donation must be handed over to the Public Offices Commission.

Statements of donations required of public companies, building societies, trade unions and similar bodies

Trade unions, financial institutions, building societies and public companies are required by the Electoral Act 1997 to publish in their annual returns any donations above £4,000 which they make to any political party, candidate or member of the Oireachtas or the European Parliament.

The name, address and description of the person or party to whom the donation is given and the value of each donation must be detailed. Where more than one donation is given to one person or party in any year, and the total of all the donations to that person or party exceeds £500 or £4,000 respectively, that too must be revealed. The donations must be totalled and treated as one donation.

What constitutes a declarable political donation?

A donation is defined in the Electoral Act 1997 to include:

- a donation of money;

- a donation of property or goods;

- conferring the right to use property or goods (without payment or consideration);

- the supply of a service free *gratis*;

- the difference between the commercial price and the price actually charged for a good, property or service or the use of a good or property;

- a contribution made in connection with a fund-raising event.

Where a service or good is provided at below the commercial rate, the difference between the reduced rate and the commercial rate is deemed to be a donation. If, for example, a printer provides 10,000 canvass cards to a Dáil candidate for a fee of £8,000 where the commercial price for the printing of such cards would be £10,000 then the printer is deemed to have made a donation of £2,000 to the candidate.

Where an individual pays to attend a political fund-raising event the part of the payment that represents a net profit on the event to the party is deemed to be a donation. If, for example, a person attends a political dinner dance and pays £100 for the ticket and, after the meal, facilities and event costs, the political party makes a net profit of £50 on each ticket, £50 represents the value of the donation.

What does not constitute a declarable political donation?

The following are defined by the 1997 Act as not being declarable donations:

- free postage facilities provided to candidates in Dáil and European elections;

- party political broadcast time provided to parties or candidates;

- facilities, services or payments provided to Oireachtas or European Parliament members by reason of their office by the European Union or other intergovernmental organisations;

- assistance or services, including the use of a motor car, provided free by a person when those services are not normally part of that person's employment or business;

- coverage, by way of articles or editorial in the media, which are not advertising.

In addition, the Electoral (Amendment) Act 1998, by way of clarification, excluded two further items from the definition of donations, namely:

- benefits derived from a service rendered by the staff of a political party on behalf of the party's candidate, provided the staff are not in receipt of an extra reward or benefit in kind for the service;

- expenditure by a political party on behalf of its candidate at the election.

Distinguishing between a donation to a candidate and to a party

In order to clarify confusion which had arisen under the 1997 Act, the Electoral (Amendment) Act 1998 established a basis for determining whether a donation is regarded as having been made to election candidates and public representatives or to the political party of which they are members. The Act provided that TDs, Senators, MEPs, or unsuccessful candidates do not have to declare a donation which, although received by them, is passed on by them to the party. However, the candidate must get a written acknowledgement from the party that they have passed it on. The donation then becomes a donation to the party and is not declarable by the candidate. It is declarable by the party in the normal way if it exceeds the £4,000 threshold.

Anonymous donations

The Electoral Act 1997 makes it illegal for a political party or a Dáil, Seanad or European election candidate or their representatives to accept an anonymous donation of over £100. Where such a donation is received, it must be forwarded within fourteen days to the Public Offices Commission.

The Act also makes it illegal for a candidate in a presidential election to accept an anonymous donation of £100 or more. In this instance, details of the anonymous donation must be included in the declaration of donations which the presidential candidate is required to make and the donation must at the same time be remitted to the Public Offices Commission.

This provision is designed to prevent a situation where a candidate or donor seeks to thwart the restrictions on giving or receiving donations by giving them anonymously. Where a person fails to declare and forward an anonymous donation to the Public Offices Commission within the time limit, he may be liable on summary conviction to a fine of up to £1,000 and a further fine of £100 for each day the failure continues.

Offences and penalties

Where a candidate, Oireachtas member, MEP, political party, agent or officer fails to make the required declaration statement, he is liable on summary conviction to a fine of up to £1,000. Where he knowingly furnishes a declaration statement that fails to disclose a donation above £500 and £4,000 as appropriate, he can be liable on conviction on indictment to a fine of up to £20,000 and/or a prison sentence of up to three years.

The offences and penalties pertaining to the combined election expenditure and donation statement made by local authority candidates are outlined at Chapter 12 above.

16 Miscellaneous Campaign Law

Candidates' entitlement to free postage

Extent of the entitlement
Candidates in Dáil, European and presidential elections as well as candidates standing on the university panel in Seanad elections are entitled to post one item free of charge to each elector.[1] The entitlement extends to candidates in Dáil by-elections and Seanad by-elections on the university panel. There is no provision made for free postage facilities to candidates in local elections or to Seanad election candidates other than those nominated on the university panels.

The entitlement to free postage is set out, in similar terms, in the legislation governing each election. Section 57 of the Electoral Act 1992 in respect of Dáil elections provides that:

> Each candidate at a Dáil election shall, subject to conditions as may be specified in regulations made under section 74 of the Postal and Telecommunications Services Act 1983, be entitled to send free of charge for postage to each person on the register of the Dáil Electors for the constituency or to any combination of such persons, one postal communication containing matter relating to the election only and not exceeding 50 grammes in weight.

It is for the candidate to choose whether to send one communication to each elector or to each household or any such combination of electors.

The 1992 Act goes on to provide that where two or more candidates in a constituency are candidates of the same political party then, for the purpose of this free postage entitlement, those candidates are regarded as a single candidate. Consequently, each party is only entitled to one free postal communication to each elector in the constituency even if they have more than one candidate standing in that election.

1.　See, for example, section 57, Electoral Act 1992 and section 22, European Parliament Elections Act 1997.

If a person is a candidate in more than one constituency, then the candidate is entitled to free postage in respect of one constituency only. The candidate must state in writing the constituency for which he wishes to avail of the entitlement.

In all these elections the candidate can only exercise this right to free postage after he is validly nominated, unless he is prepared to give An Post security against the cost of postage of the item should his nomination not be accepted or be withdrawn

Specifications and posting arrangements
The reference in this section (and in the similarly worded sections relating to the other elections) to the fact that the entitlement to free postage is conferred subject to conditions specified by regulation is significant. A regulation is made in respect of each election and lays down rules governing the arrangements regarding the shape and size of the communication, the delivery of the communication to An Post, and other items.

The maximum weight of the postal communication is laid down in statute and is the same for all elections. It is currently fixed at 50 grammes, which corresponds to post to which the standard postage rates apply. The regulations specify that the words 'Litir um Thoghchán' or 'Election Communication' must be printed or stamped on the communication, or, if it is in an envelope, on the face of the envelope. The 1999 European Election Regulation,[2] which was consistent with previous regulations, specified that the communication should not exceed 235mm in length and 120mm in width.

The 1999 Regulation also specified that the election communication should, unless otherwise permitted, be posted in the elector's local postal district, be faced the same way up, tied in bundles of 120 and, as far as possible, be sorted according to streets or districts. An Post is under no obligation to deliver wrongly or insufficiently addressed communications.

Content
The question of what the election communication can contain and what amounts to "matter relating to the election" was judicially considered in *Dillon v Minister for Post and Telegraphs*[3]

Oireachtas envelopes
The statutory right to one free postage item per candidate/party in elections is distinct from the free postage facilities in the form of Oireachtas

---

2.   SI No.312 of 1993.
3.   See page 155. See also Dr Eamonn Hall, "Dishonest Politicians" *Law Gazette*, (1999).

envelopes available to outgoing TDs and senators. This service is available on an ongoing basis and derives from their membership of the Oireachtas.

Legal requirements regarding election literature

All election material must have on its face the name of the printer and the publisher. The publisher is usually either the candidate himself, his agent or the party director of elections.

The requirement extends to "every printed material, bill, poster or similar document having reference to an election or distributed for the purpose of furthering the candidature of any candidate at an election".

Failure to include the printer and publisher details on election literature is an electoral offence. It is punishable, on summary conviction, by a fine of up to £1,000 and/or imprisonment for up to six months and, on conviction on indictment, to a fine of up to £2,500 and a prison sentence of up to two years.[4]

The 1992 Act provides that "anyone who prints, publishes or posts, or causes to be printed, published or posted any such literature or poster without the printer and publishers details may be found guilty of this offence". Posting in this instance refers to the act of displaying or "putting up" a poster rather than mailing.

Election postering and the Litter Acts

The law provides for a temporary exemption from litter-related provisions and penalties for posters that are erected during the course of an election or referendum campaign.

Section 19 of the Litter Pollution Act 1997 provides that a person shall be guilty of an offence, prosecuted by the local authority, where he exhibits or causes to be exhibited any article or advertisement on any structure, door, gate, window, tree, pole or post is on or is visible from a public place, where he is not the owner. However, section 19(7) provides that a prosecution shall not be brought where an offence under this section is alleged to have been committed in respect of an advertisement that relates to a presidential or general election, a by-election, local election, referendum or European election, unless the advertisement has been in position for seven days or longer after the latest day for which the poll was taken for the election concerned.

In effect, therefore, election posters are not illegal under the Litter Pollution Act 1997 during the election campaign period. Parties and candidates are given seven days grace in which to remove the posters. If they

---

4. See section 140, Electoral Act 1992.

fail to do so in that time, they are first served with a notice under the Act specifying the location where posters are still in breach and if these are still not removed then the party, agent and or candidate can be prosecuted in the District Court and if convicted face a fine in respect of each breach.

Prohibition on campaigning at polling stations

The 1992 Act introduced a prohibition on political campaigning of any type (canvassing, postering, literature or loudspeakers) in any polling station, in the ground of any polling station and within 100 yards of any polling station.

The prohibition applies from 30 minutes before polling commences until 30 minutes after polls close. The section specifically defines the polling station to include all parts of the building and any land within the curtilage of the building within which the polling station is situated. The distance of 100 yards is measured from any entrance to the polling station or its grounds.

The following is prohibited:

- loitering or congregating with other persons;

- attempting to induce by any means whatsoever an elector to vote for a candidate or vote in a particular way or to refrain from voting;

- displaying or distributing any notice, sign or poster (other than one displayed by the returning officer) or card or circular or other document relating to the election;

- using or causing to be used any loud speaker or other public address mechanism to broadcast matter relating to the election.

Broadcasting legislation and the coverage of elections and referenda

Impartiality

The legislative provisions governing RTÉ and the coverage of election campaigns is the same as that which governs the station's obligation of impartiality in all current affairs. They are set out at section 18(1) of the Broadcasting Authority Act 1960, as amended by section 3 of the Broadcasting Authority (Amendment) Act 1976. It provides:

> Subject to subsection 1(a) of this section, it shall be the duty of the [RTÉ] Authority to ensure that:

17 Referendum Law

Calling of referenda

Referenda in Ireland are usually held to enable the people to decide whether or not to amend a particular Article or section of the Constitution.[1] There is provision in the Constitution for a referendum on proposals other than a proposal to amend the Constitution. This alternative type of referendum is referred to in the Referendum Act 1994 as an "ordinary" referendum.[2]

Ordinary referenda

The Constitution lays down the following procedure for the calling of an ordinary referendum.

The President must receive a petition from a simple majority of the members of the Seanad and not less than one third of the members of the Dáil requesting that a specified bill be referred to the people for their approval by way of a referendum. If the President, following consultation with the Council of State, decides that the bill contains a proposal of such national importance that the will of the people thereon ought to be ascertained before the measure becomes law, one of the following must happen: a referendum is held on the proposal or a general election is held. If a general election is not called and the referendum is held, the bill is deemed to have been vetoed by the people if the majority of the votes are cast against the proposal and such votes represent at least one-third of the presidential electors on the register of electors.

Constitutional referendum

In order for a constitutional referendum to be called, a proposal to amend the Constitution must be introduced in the Dáil as a bill. When the bill has been passed by both houses of the Oireachtas, it must be submitted to the people for approval at a referendum. If a majority of the votes cast at the referendum is in favour of the proposal, the bill is signed by the president and the Constitution is amended accordingly.

---

1. See Article 46 and Article 47.
2. For the law relating to referenda, see the Electoral Act 1992, the Referendum Act 1994, the Electoral (Amendment) Act 1996 and the Referendum Act 1998.

Conduct of referenda

The procedures for the holding of constitutional and ordinary referenda are broadly similar.

The Minister for the Environment appoints the polling day, which must be between 30 and 90 days after the making of the order. The Minister also designates the hours of opening for the poll, which must be at least twelve hours between 8.30 am and 10 pm.

The Minister appoints a referendum returning officer, who is responsible for the overall conduct of the referendum.[3] The Dáil constituency returning officers act as local returning officers and organise the conduct of the poll and the count in each constituency. The procedure for the organisation and the conduct of the poll (with the exception of the appointment of agents) is the same as in elections.[4] The procedure for the issue of ballot papers to ordinary, postal and special voters is also the same.[5]

The polling stations are the same as for a Dáil election, and a polling card must be sent to each elector. The polling card must include the elector number as detailed on the register of electors and, in this instance, should also include a formal statement prescribed by the Oireachtas regarding the subject matter of the referendum. This explanatory statement must be displayed prominently at each polling station. A full copy of the bill containing the proposal to amend the Constitution must be available at post offices and other public buildings for free inspection and for purchase at a nominal price.

Eligibility to vote in referenda

Every citizen of Ireland who is at least 18 years of age and whose name appears on the register of electors is entitled to vote at a referendum. Although nationals of the United Kingdom and of other Member States of the European Union may be entitled to vote in Dáil, European and local elections, they are not entitled to vote in referenda. A person may vote only once in a referendum.

Voting procedure and the format of the ballot paper

Voting is by secret ballot, and the format of the ballot paper for referendum is prescribed by law. The ballot paper must contain brief instructions on the correct manner of voting. The actual text of the amendment to the

---

3. Usually an official of the franchise section in the Department of the Environment.
4. See Chapter 4 on Organisation of the Poll.
5. See Chapter 3 on Voting Procedures.

Constitution does not appear. Instead, the ballot paper shows the title of the bill proposing to amend the Constitution and asks whether the elector approves of the passing of this bill. The voter marks an 'X' in either the 'yes' or the 'no' box on the ballot paper.

Returning officers and organisation of the poll
The procedure for the organisation and the conduct of the poll (with the exception of the appointment of agents) is the same as in elections. The procedure for the issue of ballot papers to ordinary, postal and special voters is also the same. (See Chapters 5 to 9 above)

The Referendum Commission
The Referendum Act 1998 provides for the establishment of an independent statutory referendum commission, which has two functions.

Functions
First, the referendum commission prepares and disseminates information on the subject matter of a referendum, and fosters and promotes and, where appropriate, facilitates public debate on the referendum in a manner that is fair to all interests concerned at a referendum.

Second, the referendum commission considers and rules on applications from bodies to be deemed approved bodies and thereby become entitled to appoint agents at the referendum.

Establishment
A new referendum commission comes into being in respect of each referendum. The referendum commission in each case is established by order of the Minister for the Environment. This ministerial order must be made, in the case of a constitutional referendum, not earlier than the day on which the bill amending the Constitution is initiated in Dáil Éireann. In the case of an ordinary referendum, the ministerial order establishing the commission must be made not later than the date of the making of the order appointing the polling date for such referendum.

Membership
The chairperson of the referendum commission in each case must be a former judge of the Supreme Court or a serving or former judge of the High Court nominated by the Chief Justice. The other four members are the

---

6. In the case of the Comptroller and Auditor General, the Ombudsman, the Clerk of the Dáil and the Clerk of the Seanad there is provision for the officeholder's deputy to serve on the commission where the office is vacant or the office holder is otherwise incapacitated.

Comptroller and Auditor General, the Ombudsman, the Clerk of the Seanad and the Clerk of the Dáil.[6]

The commission is required to act independently and regulates its own procedures. The facilities and staff required by the commission are provided by the Department of Finance. The commission can hire consultants or agencies to assist in its work.

Information activities of the Referendum Commission

The principal information function of the commission is to prepare one or more statements containing a general explanation of the subject matter of the referendum and to prepare one or more statements setting out the arguments for and against the proposal and to publish and distribute these to the electorate.

In the referenda since its inception, the referendum commission has fulfilled this function using press advertisements and leaflets and brochures delivered directly to homes. Some of these gave general information about the referendum proposals and others contained arguments for and against the proposals.

The 1998 Act provides that the prohibition against the acceptance of political advertising does not apply to advertisements to be broadcast at the request of the referendum commission as part of its functions. The Minister for Arts, Heritage, Gaeltacht and the Islands can direct both RTÉ and the IRTC to make broadcasting time available to facilitate the referendum commission in the performance of its functions.

Appointment of personation and count agents

Each member of both Houses of the Oireachtas has the right to appoint agents to act as personation agents, to attend at the issuing and opening of postal ballots and to attend at the counting of votes in a referendum.[7] Members of the Dáil can appoint such agents to polling stations and count centres in respect of the constituency they represent. The right of members of the Seanad to appoint agents extends to all polling stations and count centres throughout the country.

The Referendum Act 1998 extends the right to appoint these agents to organisations, which are deemed to be 'approved bodies' by the referendum commission. A body must apply at each referendum at which it wishes to appoint agents. The referendum commission is required to publish a notice in the national newspapers giving details of the procedure for bodies wishing to apply to become approved bodies for the referendum.

---

7.   See *Sherwin v The Minister for the Environment,* page 172.

The requirements for a body to be declared an approved body are relatively straightforward. The body must:

- have a bona fide interest in the subject matter of the referendum;

- be organised in the State;

- have at least 500 members;

- have a constitution, memorandum of association or other such document; and

- have a name that is not identical to or does not closely resemble the name of a registered political party.

The commission can seek further information from a body when considering its application. It is an offence to knowingly provide false information to the commission in making such an application, and a declaration as an approved body can be revoked if false information has been furnished to it. Having made its decision, the referendum commission must notify the referendum returning officer of the details of each body that it declares to be an approved body. Each approved body is then invited to appoint agents to attend at the issuing and opening of postal ballot papers, at polling stations and at the counting of votes.

Arrangements for the referendum count
The count begins at 9 am on the day following the poll (or a day or more later if an election is held on the same day). If two or more referenda are held on the same day the ballot papers for both referenda can be sorted and counted together. The local returning officer conducts the count locally at a constituency count centre and forwards the result to the referendum officer at the national count centre.

Declaration of the result
Once the referendum returning officer has received the final result from all constituencies, he draws up a provisional referendum certificate stating the overall result of the voting and indicating whether or not the proposal has been approved. This certificate is published in *Iris Oifigiúil*. Within seven days after formal publication, any elector may apply to the High Court for leave to present a petition questioning the provisional

certificate.[8] If no petition is presented, the certificate becomes final. If the final certificate shows that the majority of the votes cast were in favour of the proposal, the relevant bill is signed by the President, and the Constitution is amended accordingly.

---

8.   See Chapter 18 on Election and Referendum Petitions.

18 Election and Referendum Petitions

Dáil election petitions
A Dáil election can only be questioned by a petition to the High Court. The procedure for the presenting and trial of petitions challenging a Dáil election in any constituency are laid down at section 132 of the Electoral Act 1992 and in Schedule III to that Act as amended by section 44 of the Electoral Act 1997.[1]

The petitioner
A Dáil election petition may be presented by the Director of Public Prosecutions (DPP) or any person who is registered or entitled to be registered as a Dáil elector in the relevant Dáil constituency.

Unless the petition is presented by the DPP, it must be accompanied by a lodgement of £5,000 as security against costs. The court can waive or reduce this amount where it is of the opinion that the petitioner is unable to lodge the required amount or that it would cause him serious hardship to do so. A Dáil election petition must be presented by lodging it in the High Court central office.

Time limit

- In the normal course of events, a petition must be lodged within 28 days of the declaration of the result by the returning officer.

- Where the petition alleges bribery and where it is specifically alleged that the bribe was made or passed after the declaration of the result, the petition must be presented within 28 days after the day this is alleged to have happened.

- The Electoral Act 1997 provides that where the petition alleges an irregularity or non-compliance with election expenditure controls, then, even if a petition may already have been presented in relation

---

1. See Order 97 of the Rules of the Superior Courts for the procedure generally as regards parliamentary petitions.

to that election, a petition can be brought within seven days after the laying of a copy of the relevant election expense statement before the Oireachtas.

Format of the petition

The petition must be dated and signed by the petitioner and must specify the Dáil election to which it relates, the grounds on which it is presented, the remedy it seeks and the name and address of the petitioner and his solicitor.

In addition to lodging a copy of the petition in the central office, a copy of the petition must also be served on:

- any person to whose election it relates;

- the Minister for the Environment;

- the Clerk of the Dáil;

- the returning officer for the constituency to which it relates;

- where not presented by the DPP, to the DPP.

The returning officer is required to publish notice of the petition in the constituency.

Grounds for challenging a Dáil election

A Dáil election may be questioned on one or more of the following grounds:

- want of eligibility (of a candidate to contest the election);

- the commission of a criminal offence referred to in Part XXII of the 1992 Act;

- obstruction or interference with or other hindrance of the conduct of the election;

- mistake or other irregularity in the conduct of the election, which if established is likely to have affected the result of the election.

Trial of the petition

When the High Court hears a petition, it does so as a divisional court of three judges. Each year, the President of the High Court nominates three High Court judges to be placed on the rota for the trial of election petitions. The court is obliged, when fixing a date for the trial of a Dáil petition, to deal with the matter as soon as is reasonably possible.

Once the date for the trial of the petition is fixed, the Clerk of the Dáil, unless otherwise ordered by the courts, before the trial delivers to the central office the packets of ballot papers, reports of the returning officer, ballot paper accounts, tendered votes lists, packets of counterfoils and marked copies of the register. The central office retains these safely until the trial is over.

The returning officer is also required, notwithstanding the fact that he may be a witness or party to the proceedings to give the court any assistance requested.

The court can hear oral evidence from any witness.

Court-directed re-count

If it feels it necessary as part of the trial of the petition, the court can order under its direction the counting afresh of all votes cast at the election in the constituency to which the petition relates. Alternatively, the court can choose only to count particular bundles afresh. In conducting such a recheck, the court can reverse any decision of the returning officer at the original count. The court can also disregard preferences recorded on ballot papers which are spoiled, preferences recorded on forged or counterfeit ballot papers and preferences recorded for any person who is found by the court not to have been eligible for election.

Case stated or appeal on a point of law to the Supreme Court

At any stage of the trial of a petition, the court may on its own motion or on the application of any party to the petition, state a case for the opinion of the Supreme Court in any point of law arising at the trial.

Form of a court order arising from a Dáil election petition

Having heard the petition, the High Court can:

- dismiss the petition;
- make orders substituting what it has found to be the correct result of the election for the one initially declared;

- if it considers that it is unable to determine the correct result declare the election, or part of it, void.

Consequences of a court order arising from a Dáil election petition
Where, as a result of the court order, a person who had initially been declared elected to the Dáil is now deemed not to be duly elected, they cease to be a member from the day after the Clerk of the Dáil is notified of the court's decision. Notwithstanding this, anything done by the person now ceasing to be a member of the Dáil, including voting or participating in the Dáil is still deemed valid.

Where the court declares the whole or part of an election in a constituency void, a fresh election is then held to fill the resulting Dáil vacancy or vacancies. Therefore, if a petition was taken against the manner in which the poll election or count was conducted in a five-seat constituency, the High Court could find the whole of the election in that constituency void and therefore all five seats would be filled by a by-election.

Alternatively, the Court might find that only the last seat was filled incorrectly, accordingly, the election of the fifth person deemed elected would be void and a by-election would be held to fill that vacancy. The result in the other 40 constituencies would not be affected and the Dáil would continue in existence with the vacancy (or vacancies) until the by-election was held.

The 1992 Act specifies that the by-election to fill vacancies arising from an electoral petition must be held not later than three months after the court order, unless the Dáil has less than six months of its term still to run.

Presidential election petitions
A presidential election result may only be questioned by petition to the High Court. The procedure for the presenting of presidential election petitions are very much similar to those for Dáil elections, and are set out at sections 57 and 58 of the Presidential Elections Act 1993. The 1993 Act specifies that the provisions of Schedule III of the Electoral Act 1992 pertaining to Dáil election petitions shall also apply to presidential petitions.[2]

Leave of the court to present a petition
A petition to a presidential election cannot be lodged without the purported petitioner first having received leave from the High Court to present such a petition. The High Court is required by the Act to give priority to a presidential election petition over any other business. The Act specifies that the Court shall not grant leave to present such a petition unless is satisfied

---

2. To date, no presidential election petition has been tried.

that that there is prima facie evidence of the defect or interference on which the petitions advanced and, secondly, that the defect or interference is such as to have materially affected the result of the election.

Time limit
The application for leave to present the petition must be made not later than seven days after the declaration by the presidential returning officer of the result of the election. The time limit is extended to seven days after an alleged bribe when an allegation of a bribe paid after polling day is the basis of the petition.

The petitioner
The group of persons entitled to petition a presidential election is narrower than all other polls. Only the DPP, or a candidate in the presidential election or his or her election agent is entitled to present such a petition.

Again, the petitioner must provide the required £5,000 security against costs unless otherwise ordered by the court. In addition to the Minister for the Environment, the presidential returning officer and the DPP, a presidential election petition must be served on any local returning officer concerned and all candidates in the presidential election.

The grounds for challenging a presidential election
The presidential election may be questioned on the same grounds as a Dáil election:

- want of eligibility;

- the commission of an electoral offence under the 1992 Act;

- obstruction of or interference with or other hindrance to the conduct of the election; or

- mistake or other irregularity,

which if established are likely to have affected the result of the election.

Trial of the petition
As with other petitions, the High Court sits as a divisional court, when hearing a petition. The presidential returning officer hands over the ballot papers and document to the central office and the court may order the votes

to be re-counted under its direction. Again, there is provision for a case to be stated to the Supreme Court on a point of law.

Form and consequences of a court order arising out of a presidential election petition
Having heard the petition, the court can:

- dismiss the petition;

- uphold the result as announced by the presidential returning officer;

- declare what the court has found to be the correct result of the election;

- declare that the presidential election or a specified part of it was void.

Where the Court declares the presidential election void a fresh election is held and the Minister must as soon as may be make a new presidential election order.

Where the court declares part of the election void the election is taken again in the relevant constituency or part of the constituency as the courts directs. The Court sets the date on which this partial election must be held.

European election petitions
The legislative provisions relating to European election petitions are set out in the main at section 21 of the European Parliament Elections Act 1997.[3]

As with other election petitions, the leave of the High Court must be obtained before a European election petition can be presented. The application must be made to the Court not later than seven days after the declaration by the returning officer of the result. The time limit is extended to seven days after an alleged bribe if such a bribe after polling day forms the basis of the petition.

Petitioner
The petition can be brought be any person on the register of electors in the relevant European constituency or by the DPP. Once leave is obtained, the petition must be lodged with the central office. The petitioner must provide security for costs unless otherwise ordered by the Court.

---

3. *Dell v Fitzsimons,* see page 152.

Trial of the petition
The trial is heard by a divisional court of the High Court, any witnesses can be called and the Court has the usual powers to order a re-count of the votes under its direction. There is again provision for an appeal to the Supreme Court on a point of law.

Form and consequences of a court order arising from a petition
Having heard the petition, the Court can:

- dismiss the petition;

- substitute what it has found to be the correct result of the election; or

- declare the election in that European constituency or a specified part of it to be void.

Where an election or part of it in a European constituency is declared void, a fresh election must be held on a date appointed by the minister, which must be not later than three months after the date of the court order. It is not obligatory to hold the fresh election if another European election is due within six months following the court order.

Local election petitions
The provisions governing local election petitions are set out in the Local Elections (Petitions and Disqualifications) Act 1974.[4] The procedure is similar to that for Dáil election petitions with the following key distinctions.

Circuit Court
Local election petitions are presented to and heard by the Circuit Court rather than the High Court. A petition can be presented by any person over the age of 18 (or the DPP) and is presented by lodging it in the office of the county registrar for the county in which the principal office of the relevant local authority is situated. The petition must be tried by a judge of the Circuit Court assigned for the time being to that circuit and the trial must take place in that county.

Time limit
A local election petition must be presented within 28 days of the result of

---

4. *Byrne v Allen*, see page 153.

the election being declared except, as in the other elections, where bribery is alleged when the deadline is later. The petitioner is required to lodge a security for costs.

In order to be lodged with the court, a copy of the petition must be given to each person to whose election it relates, to the Minister for the Environment, to the Secretary or Clerk of the relevant local authority and, except where the petition is presented by the DPP, to the DPP.

The grounds for questioning a local election are the same: want of qualification, obstruction interference with the poll, or mistake or other irregularity, which, if established, are likely to effect the result of the election.

The trial of the petition

The Circuit Court, when setting a date for the trial of the petition, must deal with the matter as soon as is reasonably possible. The court can call any witnesses and can order under its supervision a full or partial re-count of the votes cast. The Circuit Court can on its own motion or on the application of any party state a case on a point of law to the Supreme Court.

The form and consequences of a court order arising out of a local election petition

Having heard the petition, the Circuit Court judge can dismiss it, substitute the declared result with one which the court finds, to be the correct one or, if it considers that is unable to determine the correct result it can order that the entire election or a specified part of it is void.

Where, as a result of a petition, a person originally declared elected is deemed not to have been elected, they cease to be a member of the local authority the day after the order is notified to the clerk or secretary. They also cease to be member of any other local body to which they were appointed by the local authority. Anything they did while a member of the authority, including anything done as a chairman of the authority if he were so elected, remains valid.

Where the Court declares part of an election void, the vacancy created is deemed a casual vacancy and is filled by co-option in the normal way. However, where, as a result of the court order, the number of persons validly elected in an electoral area is less than the majority of such members the election is deemed not to have taken place and a new election takes place in that electoral area. Where the court determines that the whole election was void or the number of members of persons validly elected to membership of the local authority is less than a quorum, a new election is held.

The Electoral Act 1997 and election petitions

The Electoral Act 1997 introduced an amendment to each of the acts dealing with the various election petitions. There are two effects of this amendment.

Firstly, where an electoral petition alleges an irregularity or non-compliance with Part VI of that Act (the election expenditure controls), then (notwithstanding that a petition may already have been presented in relation to that election) a person otherwise entitled to bring a petition can do so within seven days after the laying of a copy of the relevant statement of election expenses before each House of the Oireachtas.

Secondly, the amendment inserted specifies that the election shall not be declared invalid because of a non-compliance with any provision of Part VI of the 1997 Act, or mistake in the use of forms provided for in the Act or in any regulation made under it, where it appears to the court that the candidate complied with the principles laid down in that part of the Act, taken as a whole and that such non-compliance or mistake did not materially affect the result of the election.

Referendum petitions

The rules and procedures governing the challenging of a referendum results are laid down in the Referendum Act 1994.[5] It is different from that governing a Dáil election petition in a number of respects.

Time limit

Following on from the count, the referendum returning officer prepares the provisional referendum certificate showing the votes cast in favour and against the proposed amendment. A copy of that certificate is then published in *Iris Oifigiúil*. In the normal course the Master of the High Court informs the referendum returning officer that no or no valid petition has been made and then the certificate becomes final and incapable of being questioned.

Once the provisional referendum certificate has been published, a petitioner can seek leave from the High Court to bring a petition to challenge it. An application for leave to present a referendum commission must be made within seven days of the formal publication of the provisional certificate.

The petitioner

A referendum petition can be presented by any citizen who has reached the age of 18 years or by the Dulector of Public Prosecutions.

---

5.   See *Hanafin v Minister for the Environment* [1996] 2 ILRM 160, at page 175.

The grounds for challenging a referendum

The referendum result as set out in the provisional certificate can be questioned on one or more of the following grounds:

- the commission of an offence under the 1994 Act;

- obstruction of interference with or other hindrance to the conduct of the referendum;

- failure to complete or otherwise conduct the referendum in accordance with the 1994 Act; or

- mistake or other irregularity in the conduct of the referendum or in the particulars stated in the provisional referendum certificate.

The defect or obstruction complained of must actually have materially effected the referendum result.

Section 48 of the 1994 Act provides that the Court shall not order the referendum to be taken again in any constituency merely on account of any provision of the Act or an error in the use of forms provided in the Act where it appears to the court that the referendum was conducted in that constituency in accordance with the general principles of the Act and that the non-compliance or error did not affect the result of the referendum as a whole.

The issue of what amounts to an obstruction or interference in the referendum came under extensive judicial consideration in the *Hanafin* petition of the result of the "divorce referendum". It was said to include more than just an interference with the practical and physical conduct of the poll and could be extended to include, for example, unconstitutional activity by the government in spending public funds in advocating a particular vote in the referendum.

As is the case with electoral petitions, the trial of a referendum petition is heard by a divisional court of three judges, any witness can be called and the court can order a re-count of all or some of the votes under its direction.

Form and consequences of a court order arising from a referendum petition

Having heard the petition, the court can:

- makes a final order confirming without alteration the provisional certificate;

- direct that the certificate be amended in accordance with what the court has found the correct result to be;

- direct that the votes be re-counted or that the referendum be reheld in total or in some constituencies.

The Act provides that where the High Court rejects a petition and endorses the provisional certificate then the result becomes final and is incapable of being further questioned in any court.

Some commentators had thought that this gave no right of appeal of the High Court decision to the Supreme Court. However, in the *Hanafin* case, on hearing this point as a preliminary issue, the Supreme Court held that an appeal against such an order of the divisional High Court did lie in law to the Supreme Court.

Withdrawing a petition

The legislation in each instance specifies that an electoral or referendum petition once lodged cannot be withdrawn without leave of the court. When applying for leave to withdraw a petition, except in the case of a petition presented by the DPP, the petitioner must submit an affidavit stating the reasons for the proposed withdrawal and that to the best of that person's knowledge and belief the petition is not being withdrawn in consideration of any payment or the cesser of membership of the body to which the election related or for any other reason not stated in the affidavit.

Notice of intention to apply for leave to withdraw a petition must be published in at least two newspapers circulating in the relevant constituency/area or a national paper in the case of a referendum or presidential election petition.

The corrupt withdrawal of a petition is an offence punishable on conviction indictment to imprisonment for up to three months and/ or to a fine of up to £3,000.

On the hearing of an application to withdraw a petition, another person may apply to the court to be substituted as a petitioner and, if the court thinks fit, the court may substitute that person as a petitioner and the petition continues in the normal way.

Costs and penalties

Where, at the trial of the petition, it appears to the court that any person committed an electoral offence in relation to the relevant election, the court can order part or all of the costs of the petition to be paid by that person. In practice, costs are often awarded to unsuccessful petitioners who present an arguable case.[6]

Costs awarded against a returning officer, and the cost incurred by him in conducting a re-count under the direction of the court are paid by the Minster for Finance or relevant local authority.

---

6.   See *Hanafin v Minister for the Environment* [1996] 2 ILRM 160 and at page 175 and
     Dillon-Leetch v Calleary at page 156.

19 Ethics and Declarations of Interest

Categories of persons from whom declarations are required
The Ethics in Public Office Act 1995 provides a structure for the disclosure of interests by the following categories of people:

- Members of the Dáil, Seanad and European Parliament.

- Officeholders – this category includes ministers, ministers of state, and the Chair and deputy Chair of both the Dáil and Seanad.

- The Attorney General.

- Specified ministerial appointees – this is defined in the Act as a person employed or contracted by an officeholder personally otherwise than by means of competitive procedure. It includes persons appointed as special advisers, programme managers or personal assistants to the office holders and similarly appointed temporary established civil servants.

- Public servants – this category includes senior civil servants.

- Directors and certain employees of designated public bodies – this category includes members of the board of directors (or similar authority) and certain senior employees of public companies and authorities, which are designated as coming within the remit of this Act by regulations made by the Minister for Finance.

Disclosable interests
The Act specifies three types of interests, which are disclosable.

Registerable interests
The following are the items which are deemed by the Act and its Second Schedule to be registerable interests:

- Any other occupation, trade or profession for which more than £2,000 was received in the period covered by the return.

- Any shares, bonds or debentures or like investment in a particular company or undertaking where the aggregate value is greater than £10,000.

- A directorship or shadow directorship of a company.

- An interest in land or property (excluding the family home) where that interest exceeds £10,000.

- Any gift or combined gifts greater than £500 received, excluding personal gifts received from friends or relations.

- Property lent or services provided free of charge where the commercial value of that letting/service would be greater than £500.

- Travel facilities and hospitality (living accommodation, meals and entertainment) supplied outside the State where it was provided otherwise than by virtue of their being a member, officeholder, designated director, occupier of a designated position or special adviser or by virtue of a separate employment/occupation that they have.

- A paid position as a political or public affairs lobbyist, consultant or adviser.

- Any contract with which they were connected to supply goods or services to a minister or department or public body where the value or combined value of that contract(s) was greatest than £5,000.

Additional interests
Some of those who are required to make declarations are also required to declare additional interests. Additional interests are the registerable interests (as set out above) of a spouse or child of which an officeholder has actual knowledge, which could materially influence the officeholders in the exercise of their office functions because they or their spouse or child could substantially benefit as a result.

Material interests
Material interests are defined as arising when the performance of the duties

or functions of the person required to make the declaration could so affect the personal interest of that person (or of a connected person) as to confer significant benefit.

Connected persons

Some declarers are obliged to declare the registerable or material interests of what is described as a connected person. The definition of a connected person is to be found in section 2 of the Ethics in Public Office Act 1995. It includes:

- a spouse (other than a separated spouse, i.e. one living "separately and apart");

- a close relation, i.e. a child, parent, brother or sister or any of their spouses;

- certain trustees;

- business partners and connected or controlled companies.

Actual knowledge

A person is deemed to have "actual knowledge" of the interest if he has "actual, direct and personal knowledge" as distinct from constructive, implied or imputed knowledge, and the term includes, in relation to a fact, belief in the fact's existence the grounds for which are such that a reasonable person who is aware of them could not doubt or disbelieve that the fact exists.

Annual Disclosures Statements

Members of the Dáil, Seanad or European Parliament
Every member of the Dáil and Seanad, (including those who are ministers and ministers of state or Attorney General) must furnish an annual written declaration of their own registerable interests to the Clerk of the Dáil and Clerk of the Seanad, as appropriate, within 30 days of the registration date. Each clerk establishes a register (known as the Register of Interests of Members of Dáil Éireann/Seanad Éireann) which it furnishes to the Public Offices Commission.

TDs and Senators are only required to declare their own interests. They are not required to include the interests of connected persons unless they are an officeholder. (See below.)

The Public Offices Commission has interpreted the legislation as requiring members of the Dáil, the Seanad and the European Parliament to make the declaration even where they have no registerable interest to declare. It is not necessary to specify the amount of monetary value of the interest or the remuneration of any outside occupation declared.

The first registration date in any Dáil is 30 days after the general election. Subsequent registration dates occur on the same date each year until the next general election.

The Clerk of each House prepares an annual register in which each clerk records every declaration received is recorded. This Register of Members Interests is laid before the House and a copy is published in *Iris Oifigiúil.*

The 1997 Act also requires that each House of the Oireachtas establishes a Select Committee on Members' Interests. In addition to having power to investigate breaches of the requirement to declare interests, the committee must publish mandatory guidelines on how declarations are to be completed and provide advice to members on the interests that are declarable.

Officeholders
In addition to the above declarations, which they are required to submit as ordinary members of the Oireachtas, officeholders have an obligation to disclose to the relevant clerk any additional interest, which could materially influence the officeholder in the performance of the functions of their office.

The officeholder is required to declare those interests of spouses or children of which they have actual knowledge and the interest must be one that could materially influence the officeholder.

The declaration must be made within 30 days of the registration date to the Clerk of the Dáil or Seanad as appropriate. These declarations are not published, but the clerk is required to send a copy of the confidential declaration to the Public Offices Commission and, in the case of a minister or minister of state, to the Taoiseach.

The Attorney General
An Attorney General, who is not a member of either the Dáil or the Seanad, must furnish to the Taoiseach and to the Public Offices Commission an annual statement of any registerable or additional interest, which could materially influence him in the performance of the function of the office.

Ministerial appointees
The relevant ministerial appointees are obliged to make an annual statement of their registerable and additional interests, which could materially influence

them in the exercise of their duties. The declaration in this instance is made to the relevant minister and to the Public Offices Commission.

Civil servants, designated directors and designated officeholders
Senior civil servants and members are obliged to make an annual disclosure statement of any registerable or additional interest which could materially influence them in the exercise of their duties. Senior civil servants usually furnish their statement to the Secretary General of the department. The annual declarations of civil servants are not furnished to the Public Offices Commission.

Directors of designated public bodies and designated officeholders must furnish a disclosure statement to a person within the body – normally the company secretary or equivalent – and to the Public Offices Commission. Where the person holds a designated position within a designated public body then the annual disclosure statement is furnished to the person within the body only.

Disclosure statement of a material interest in the performance of a function

The Ethics in Public Office Act 1995 lays down a complicated procedure to deal with circumstances where an officeholder may have a conflict of interest in a matter that is relevant to his duties, or where he has an interest in something about which he is making representations to another officeholder.

Officeholders and public servants covered by the Act are required, in addition to their annual statements, to make a disclosure in the form of a statement of a material interest in circumstances where their performance of certain functions affects a material interest on their own part or on the part of a person connected to them.

The officeholder must prepare the statement of a material interest setting out the facts and the nature of the material interest and furnish it to a number of persons depending on the office held.

- The Taoiseach furnishes a statement of material interest to the Chairman of the Public Offices Commission.

- A minister or minister of state or an Attorney General furnishes a statement of material interest to the Taoiseach and to the Public Offices Commission.

- The Chair or Deputy Chair of the Dáil or Seanad furnishes a statement of material interest to the Public Offices Commission.

- A director of a designated public body furnishes a statement of material interest to the other directors.

- A holder of a designated position in a designated body furnishes a material interest statement to their relevant board.

- Ministerial appointees are required to furnish the statement to their minister and to the Public Offices Commission.

Declarations during the course of Oireachtas proceedings

Oireachtas members, including ministers and ministers of state, when speaking in a Dáil or Seanad debate on an issue in which they, or a 'connected person', has a material interest, must declare that interest in the House before or during their speech.

Where an Oireachtas member is not speaking but is voting in the House on an issue in which he, or a connected person, has a material interest he must, prior to the vote, give a written declaration of this interest to the clerk of the House.[1] This declaration must be published in any official reports of proceedings of the relevant House. Where the issue is being discussed in a committee of the Houses of the Oireachtas, the declaration should be made to the clerk of the committee.

Such declarations are not required where the interest in question has already been declared in the member's annual declaration.

Declaration and forfeiture of gifts

The Ethics in Public Office Act 1995 lays down a specific procedure, which must be followed by officeholders when they or their spouses or children receive gifts or are provided with property or services free or at a rate less than the commercial value, where the value of such gifts, property or services exceeds £500. The Act's provisions are amplified by guidelines for officeholders published by the government on 14 August 1996.

A gift for the purpose of the Act includes:

- a gift of money or other property;

- the provision of a service free of charge;

- the provision of a service or property at below commercial rate;

- a loan of property free of charge or for less than its commercial value.

---

1. In May 2000 Denis Foley TD was suspended from Dáil Eireann for 14 sitting days, having admitted to a breach of this requirement following a complaint to the Committee on Members Interests.

Where a gift of money or other property which has a value greater then £500 is given to an officeholder or his spouse or child, by virtue of the office, it is deemed to be a gift given to the State and must be surrendered to the State. The officeholder must notify the Secretary General to the Government, who, if it is not already clear, determines the value of the gift and/or the question of whether it was given by virtue of the office.

The government guidelines further specify that where a minister or minister of state, officeholder of their spouse or child is offered or supplied with a service or the use of a property free or at a reduced rate and the value of that service or the use of a property exceeds £500 then that offer must be refused. If supplied, the officeholder must notify the Secretary General to the Government and make an appropriate refund to the person supplying the benefit. The Secretary General is required to inform the Taoiseach and the Tánaiste and such other Minster as may be specified by the government. Where a refund is not practicable, they will determine an appropriate alternative action such as the donation of an equivalent amount to a voluntary body or charity. The Secretary General is required to notify the Public Offices Commission of such an occurrence and of the action taken.

Where such a property or service is offered or supplied to the Attorney General, Chair or Deputy Chair of the Dáil or Seanad, or the Chair of a Dáil, Seanad or Joint Committee, the Public Offices Commission must be notified and a refund made to the Commission or alternative action taken as the commission directs.

The Act provides for specific exemptions from the procedure regarding the surrender of gifts or the declaration and refund of supply or use of property. These exemptions include circumstances where it is given:

- as a donation for political purposes;

- for personal reasons only by a friend or relative;

- by virtue of another office or position.

Investigations by the Public Offices Commission

On receipt of a complaint, either directly or by reference from the Clerk of the Dáil or Seanad, or in some instances on its own initiative, the Public Offices Commission can undertake an investigation into a breach of the Act. In respect of certain public servants or officeholders in public bodies, the relevant minister must be consulted before the investigation is initiated.

The commission has considerable investigative powers. Its chairman may direct the person who is the subject of the investigation to attend before it, or it may direct any other person to give evidence before the commission. He may also direct the production of documents. A witness before the commission is entitled to the same privileges and immunities as a witness in the High Court. Sittings of the commission for the purpose of such investigation may be held in private.

Fair procedure
There is statutory provision for fair procedure in the conduct of the commission's investigations. The person who is the subject of a complaint is entitled to be informed of the date, time and place of the sitting of the commission. He must be provided with:

- a statement of the alleged breach;

- details of the witnesses that the commission proposes to call;

- a copy of each witness' statement;

- a written indication of the nature and source of any information available which may be favourable to him and of which he may be unaware.

The subject and complainant are entitled to be present and have legal representation at such a hearing and to cross-examine witnesses.

Report on a commission investigation
The commission is required to produce a report of its findings and determinations. Where the commission determines that there was no contravention of the 1997 Act, the report must state whether the commission is of the opinion that the complaint was frivolous, vexatious or without reasonable grounds. There is provision in such circumstance for the commission to impose costs against the complainant.

If the commission determines that there was a contravention the report must state:

- where the contravention is continuing, the steps required to be taken to secure compliance with the Act and the timescale for taking such steps;

- whether the commission is of the view that the breach was inadvertent, negligent, reckless or intentional;

- whether in all the circumstances, the contravention was serious or minor;

- whether the person acted in good faith and in the belief that his actions accorded with guidelines published or advices given in writing by a Select Committee on Members Interests or by the commission.

Where the report concerns a member of the Dáil or Seanad, it is furnished to the relevant Select Committee on Members Interests, which lays it before the House. However, generally where the breach concerns a member of the Dáil on Seanad in their activities as a member of the Dáil or Seanad (i.e. speaking or voting in the House) then it is the relevant Committee on Members Interests which undertakes the investigation. The House may take note of the report, censure the officeholder or other member concerned or suspend the officeholder or other member concerned for up to 30 days, or, if the contravention is continuing, for a longer period as may be required to secure compliance with the Act. Censure or suspension cannot be imposed if the commission's report determines that the member's act was done in good faith.

Referral to the Director of Public Prosecutions
Where the commission, during or after an investigation, becomes of the opinion that a person being investigated may have committed an offence relating to the performance of his function it must refer the matter to the Director of Public Prosecutions (DPP) for decision as to whether proceedings should be brought. The commission can be advised by the DPP to adjourn or postpone its investigation and in these circumstance may prepare an interim report.

20 Comment on Proposals for Electoral and Campaign Law Reform

The consideration of electoral law and campaign law is an underdeveloped field of study in Ireland. Although Ireland enjoys strong academic traditions in political science and electoral studies generally, there has been too little consideration of how electoral law has affected the operation and effectiveness of Ireland's political system. The rules of the game have a critical bearing on how the game is played, the strategies employed by the teams and the type of players attracted to the sport.

Changes to Irish electoral law and law that touches on politics have too often represented a knee-jerk reaction to the perceived inadequacies of politicians.

In recent years, politics as a profession has been all too sensitive about defending itself against ill-informed attack and has instead allowed itself, in an atmosphere of political correctness, to be compelled to adopt law reforms that others perceive as improving our political system.

We adopted a parliamentary political system and much of its accompanying corpus of electoral law from Britain. The one notable exception was our adoption for Dáil elections of the proportional representation single transferable vote electoral system. This corpus of law remained largely unchanged for 60 years.

In recent years, however, there has been an increasing range of legislative activism in this area. Some of the developments have been positive, including the consolidation in 1992 of many of the detailed legislative provisions governing Dáil elections and increasing consistency in the laws governing different types of elections. Many electoral practices have been codified and placed on a statutory footing. The establishment of a statutory constituencies commission is a case in point. Also notable in this context, was the 1999 referendum that gave local authorities, and the requirement of a fixed five-year term, a constitutional basis.

The other area of major legislative activity has been the introduction of legal controls and limits on political expenditure and donations. This has been a reaction to various political scandals and alleged scandals in the last decade – the investigation of some of which is still ongoing in two tribunals of inquiry.

As this book was being completed, there existed a range of proposals and reports in the political and public domain recommending further legal changes touching on electoral and campaign law. The All Party Oireachtas Committee on the Constitution has published three reports in recent years dealing with some of these issues.[1] The Joint Oireachtas Committee on Finance and General Affairs has published proposals on a working draft of a Standards in Public Office Bill and on the workings of the Public Offices Commission.[2] The Department of the Environment, for example, has published the Local Governent Bill, 2000 which includes proposals to reform various aspects of Local Government.

It is proposed to examine some of this debate about reform, and to a limited extent contribute to the debate, in this chapter under the following headings.

Reform of the Seanad

Few aspects of our political system have been the object of so many proposals for reform as Seanad Éireann. Many commentators have questioned the necessity for its existence and indeed, at one stage, it was abolished and re-established in its current form by Eamon de Valera under the 1937 Constitution.

From an electoral point of view, the most interesting proposal for reform came in the Second Progress Report of the All Party Oireachtas Committee on the Constitution.

The report recommended a single six-seat constituency from which graduates would elect senators to replace the current 'University Senators'. Such structural reform of the 'universities' dimension of the Seanad is long overdue, and has been suggested on a number of previous occasions. All political parties are on the record as favouring such reform. All that would be required is enabling legislation as the Constitution has already been amended by referendum to allow for such a change.[3] Any amending legislation should provide for a considerable broadening of the category of colleges, universities and so on whose graduates would be entitled to vote in such a restructured constituency.

The All-Party Committee also proposed that the number of members selected on the vocational panels be reduced from the current 42 to 27 and that fifteen members be elected by direct election. The vocational dimension originally intended for the Seanad does not now exist in practice and

---

1. All Party Oireachtas Committee on the Constitution, First and Second Progress Reports, April 1997.
2. The Joint Oireachtas Committee on Finance and Public Service report on government proposals for a Standards in Public Office Bill, July 1998.
3. See Article 18.4.2° at page 183.

the pretence should be removed. Again, this would not require a constitutional change, since it already provided for in the Constitution.[4] At a time when there is an increasing social partnership dimension to policy making in Ireland, it should prove possible to devise a means of ensuring that social and vocational interests represent themselves directly, rather than through party politicians in the Seanad.

The electoral system

When politicians and political commentators have reason to complain about Irish politics many of them resort to calling for changes in the electoral system. Proposals to amend the Constitution to replace the PR-STV system in Dáil elections with a 'first past the post system' were rejected by the people in referenda in 1959 and 1968. This has not deterred the occasional re-emergence of debate on replacing the system.

The All Party Oireachtas Committee on the Constitution, in its reconstituted form after the 1997 election, commissioned and published a report by Michael Laver on proposals for reform of the electoral system.[5] Laver was not convinced that the Irish electoral system should be changed, and he concluded that if it was to be changed at all, it should be to the 'additional member' proportional representation system used in Germany and New Zealand.

In July 1999, the Minister for the Environment and Local Government expressed his own preference for the introduction of such a proportional representation system – where some deputies would be elected in single seat constituencies and others would be elected from a national party list.[6] Although not as drastic as earlier proposals to introduce a first past the post system, the proposal does warrant critical evaluation.

The recommendation for single-seat constituencies has some merit. It is argued that it would mitigate the need for deputies to compete with each on an inter and intra party basis at being efficient clientelist messenger boys for their constituents. However, in the last five years deputies have been afforded additional assistance and resources to meet the demands of their constituency work. They now have their own offices in Leinster House, grants towards the establishment of constituency offices, greater

---

4. See Article 19 page 185.
5. Michael Laver, "A New Electoral System for Ireland" The Policy Institute in association with the All-Party Committee on the Constitution.
6. See Noel Dempsey TD, "The System turns TDs into Messenger Boys" *The Irish Times* (26 July 1999). See also Gene McKenna, "50 TDs to go in Reform Plan" *Irish Independent* (12 July 1999). See also support for the proposals from the Minister for Finance; Gene McKenna, "McCreevy Takes Lead as TDs Seek Pay Deal" *Irish Independent* (3 August 1999).

flexibility in the recruitment and the employment of secretarial support, allowances for telephones, including mobile phones, and computer facilities, faxes and the even the option of laptops.

It is arguable that further improvements in these facilities, staffing and support, together with building on recent improvements in the customer focus of government departments, would be a more effective means of alleviating the clientelist burden on TDs. Many have argued, and with some merit, that, far from being a burden, the clientelist function is an essential prerequisite to effective representative government in the Irish context.

The statistical analysis has shown that a switch to single-seat constituencies alone would favour the larger parties and the proportionality that is currently achieved with PR-STV would be lost. In order to alleviate this, the Minister has proposed that a number of deputies should be elected from a national list in proportion to the first preference vote their party receives. However, the introduction of such a nationally controlled list opens up a serious risk of distorting the Irish parliamentary system.

It would create two classes of deputies – one class busily servicing constituents in geographic constituencies, with the other class saved from this drudgery, supposedly to concentrate on national law-making roles. Such a system would give the party leadership and headquarters increased power, as they would decide who would be on the national list and the order in which they would appear on it. All of the main parties have increasingly centralised their candidate selection procedures by giving central committees the power to 'add on' candidates in many constituencies. Extending this power would stifle independence within parliamentary parties, which one can argue is an important component of the Irish political system where the executive arm of government has such largely unfettered power.

Political 'scrappage' schemes

The Minister also proposed that the number of TDs be reduced and that a type of voluntary redundancy scheme be introduced to pay off older deputies. This would replicate the system introduced prior to the 1999 local election whereby councillors were offered considerable payment per year of service on condition that they retire and not seek re-election.

Although there may be some merit in allowing for a turnover of public representatives and a reduction in their average age profile through a retirement scheme, the requirement that they agree not to contest the forthcoming election is constitutionally suspect. It amounts to a financial inducement from the State not to contest public office. It is arguable in light of the Supreme Court decisions in *McKenna* and *Coughlan* on equality and the use of public funds that the scheme employed for the local elections is open to constitutional challenge from those councillors who had long service but declined the financial package, contested the election and lost their seats. Any such scheme introduced for members of Dáil Éireann would be even more vulnerable to such a challenge.

The *McKenna* judgment and its consequences

In November 1995, Dublin MEP Patricia McKenna successfully challenged the constitutionality of the Department of Equality and Law Reform's plan to spend £400,000 of public funds on an advertisement campaign advocating a "Yes" vote in the "divorce referendum."[7]

Almost five years later, the Supreme Court judgment in that case still casts a long shadow. Few judgments have been as maligned, and it is arguable that few judgments have been as misrepresented.

In the aftermath of the judgment, there has been much confusion, and at times some consternation, about what the government can or cannot do in a referendum campaign. It could also be said that some have hidden behind the *McKenna* judgment as an excuse for doing nothing. Many politicians have expressed frustration at the constraints within which they say they had to operate during subsequent referenda because of the *McKenna* judgment. This frustration arises from an overly wide interpretation of the court's decision in that case.

In the *McKenna* case, the Supreme Court held by a majority of four to one that the government could not spend public funds in support of one side in a referendum. It said that such use of public money would be a breach of the constitutional right to equality and would have the effect of putting the voting rights of those citizens in favour of the amendment above those who opposed it.

The constraint imposed by the *McKenna* judgment is on the expenditure of public money in an unfair way. It does not, however, prohibit the government from providing factual information. Neither does it prohibit the government from calling for or campaigning for a "Yes" vote as long as public money is not used for this purpose. The government could campaign for a "Yes" vote by methods other than the expenditure of public moneys and that the prohibition on the use of public funds on one side did not mean that ministers were not entitled to use their State transport for example in relation to the referendum or to avail of the media to put forward their views.

---

7. *McKenna (No.2) v An Taoiseach and Others* [1995] 2 IR 10, and page 174.

This point is worth emphasising by reference to various judicial statements made in the *McKenna* judgment, and subsequently, which reinforced this point.

In his judgment in *McKenna*, Chief Justice Hamilton said that he was prepared to accept that the government is acting within its rights –

> in the giving of factual information with regard to the proposal which is the subject of the referendum, in expressing its views thereon and in urging the acceptance of such views.

Mr Justice O'Flaherty's decision in the case warned specifically against extending the consequences of the judgment. He said –

> The Government as such is entitled to campaign for the change and the individual members of the Government are entitled either in their personal, party or individual capacities to advocate the proposed change.

For the Supreme Court to have held otherwise would have been an absurdity. It would have required a Taoiseach or government ministers to maintain split personas – one as party politicians campaigning for a "Yes" or "No" vote, and another as government ministers sitting dumb on the referendum proposal. In his subsequent judgment, in the *Hanafin* petition of the divorce referendum result, Hamilton CJ took the opportunity to clarify what the Supreme Court had decided on this point in *McKenna* –

> Whilst the Supreme Court have decided that public funds may not be used to promote, or at any rate to promote in an unfair or unbalanced way, acceptance or rejection of a proposed amendment of the constitution, I do not accept that the decision of the Supreme Court in *McKenna (No.2)* prohibits the government from lending its authority to a particular view point. To my mind it would be unreal to attempt to draw a distinction between the attitude of the government and the attitude propounded by exactly the same person in a non-government capacity. Such a distinction would be beyond the boundaries of the subtle into the realms of metaphysical.

Later in the same judgment, Hamilton CJ went on to say that the constitutional impropriety identified in the *McKenna* case "lay not in the government campaigning for such a vote but that they expended public funds in so doing".

In his judgment in *Hanafin*, O'Flaherty J, reaffirming that the expenditure of public funds on an advertising campaign for a "Yes" vote was wrong, stated that he did not regard the spending of public money by a government on an opinion poll during a referendum campaign as unconstitutional.

> I hold that a government must always be entitled to gauge public opinion…and it can use the information thus gleaned to advance any particular policy that it wishes to propose to the public.

The line of judicial thinking in *McKenna* was continued in *Coughlan v IRTC & Others* where the plaintiff challenged the allocation by RTÉ of broadcast time for party political and referendum broadcasts during the divorce referendum campaign. Carney J, adopting the logic of *McKenna*, held that RTÉ could not give free airtime in an unbalanced way to one side in a referendum.

Once again, it is important to emphasise that the court did not hold that RTÉ could not give airtime for referendum broadcasts only that it must allocate such airtime freely to each side. Carney J's decision was subsequently upheld by the Supreme Court.

The basic principle behind the *McKenna* and *Coughlan* judgments is to protect the public's interest in fair debate. An overly sensitive interpretation of the judgment by politicians runs the risk of suffocating rather than assisting such debate.

The Referendum Commission

In response to the difficulties enunciated above, the government established a Referendum Commission on a legislative basis. In the context of the 1998 referenda on the Amsterdam Treaty and the Good Friday Agreement, the Commission was given the task of providing information and presenting the arguments on both sides of the two referenda. On these occasions, the commission received over £5 million of government money. Although the commission's work certainly raised the profile of the two referenda, it is questionable whether it actually raised information or knowledge levels.

In the case of the referendum of the Amsterdam Treaty, there remained considerable confusion in the public mind. This was due more to the legalistic and superficial nature of the Treaty than any failing on the part of the Referendum Commission. In the case of the Belfast Agreement, it is questionable whether the Referendum Commission was needed at all. The Northern Ireland issue dominated all media and political debate for months before the Good Friday agreement and for the weeks afterwards. The local government referendum in June 1999 was completely uncontroversial and, with the exception of the introduction of a five-year limit on the term of local authorities, contained nothing of practical substance.

It can be argued that the electorate did not need additional information in these referenda. Balanced and often bland information does not necessarily attract public interest.

If there is a failing in the legislative basis for the Referendum Commission it is that it was only given authority to engage in neutral and balanced information activity itself. It would serve the Irish political system better if it were empowered to provide a portion of money to parties or groups campaigning on each side of a referendum in equal measure as is the practise in a number of other countries. Most advertisers, television producers and political strategists would argue that passionate positions, debate and preferably 'a good row' are the best methods of ensuring greater public participation in referendum campaigns.

The limit on the power of the Oireachtas to make electoral law

Alongside *McKenna* it is arguable that the most significant court judgment touching on electoral law in Ireland is that of the Supreme Court in *In the matter of Article 26 of the Constitution and in the matter of the Electoral (Amendment) Bill 1983*.[8]

In pronouncing the judgment of the court, O'Higgins CJ stated that Article 16 of the Constitution "indicates a total code for the holding of elections to Dáil Éireann, setting out the matters which would appear to be necessary other than the minor regulatory provisions". He later said, "[V]iewed in this way, the entire provisions of Article 16 would appear to form a constitutional code for the holding of an election to Dáil Éireann, subject only to the statutory regulation of such election".

This judgment touches on, and arguably expressly restricts, the right of the legislature to make laws regulating Dáil elections. The power of the legislature pursuant to Article 16.7 is expressly made subject to the other provisions of Article 16.1 and that power has been held by the Supreme Court to relate to minor regulatory matters.

The legislature has no power to interfere with either the secret ballot or the principle of proportional representation. Similarly, it would appear that the legislature has no power to interfere with the eligibility of citizens for membership of Dáil Éireann save as provided for by Article 16.1.1° of the

---

8.　See page 161.

Constitution of Ireland. Some of these legal restrictions have been questioned by leading commentators.[9]

The candidate deposit

Another legislative provision, which is also constitutionally and morally suspect, is the deposit requirement for candidates in Dáil and European elections.[10] It is arguable that the legislature has no power to inhibit or limit a person's entitlement to contest an election by requiring this financial deposit. The requirement of a deposit is not a minor regulatory matter but is rather an inhibition on eligibility and is intended to be such. The requirement penalises an otherwise eligible citizen offering himself for election to Dáil Éireann, in the event that he does not achieve more than 25 per cent of the quota for election.[11]

It also infringes the right of the people to designate the rulers of the State as provided for by Article 6 of the Constitution of Ireland in that the intent and effect of the provision is to exclude certain eligible citizens from offering themselves to the electorate and so offends against the democratic process.[12]

The deposit requirement is also open to challenge on the grounds that it offends against the constitutional requirement for equality before the law at Article 40.1. Although the Constitution does allow discrimination, this discrimination is clearly arbitrary and unfair. It has been argued that the deposit requirement is justified in that it discourages frivolous candidates. In reality, it can only discourage some frivolous candidates, A wealthy candidate, however frivolous his candidature, would not necessarily be discouraged. It discriminates between those who have the financial resources to pay the deposit and those who have not and operates as a barrier to the candidature of anyone who is unable to come up with £300 or £1,000 as appropriate.

Under Article 40.6.1°i, the State guarantees the right of citizens to express freely their convictions and opinions. One of the ways in which citizens can express their convictions and opinions is by participation in the democratic process, as voters and/or as candidates. The deposit requirement unfairly prohibits those who have not the means to make the required deposit from contesting an election and also depriving them associated campaign and media opportunities, postage facilitates, and, in some instances, broadcasting facilities which follow from being a candidate.[13]

---

9.   See John Kelly, *The Irish Constitution* (Butterworth's, 3rd edn).
10. See sections 47 and 48, Electoral Act 1992.
11. See *Redmond v Minister for the Environment,* page 177.
12. See *McKenna v An Taoiseach*, particularly the judgment of Denham J.
13. Again, there is some support for this argument in the Denham judgment in *McKenna*.

There are a range of other mechanisms by which a candidate's intent can be tested and by which the objective of deterring frivolous candidates could be achieved without encroaching on the constitutional rights of the plaintiff to the in the manner that a deposit requirement does. One alternative would be to operate a requirement that candidates be nominated by a required number of electors (nomination by petition), a system which has operated effectively in many countries.

Appendix 1

Electoral Case Law

In the matter of the European Parliament Elections for the Constituency of Leinster: 1989
Michael Bell and Jim Fitzsimons

High Court, November 1989   *Hamilton P (presiding)*

Fianna Fáil's Jim Fitzsimons had been declared elected to the last seat in the Leinster constituency in the European election held on 15 June 1979. On the last count, Fitzsimons was just ten votes ahead of Labour's Michael Bell who then took this petition.

At issue in the petition were a number of ballot papers, which the returning officer had, at her discretion, deemed to be invalid. A Dáil election had been held on the same day as the European election. Among the ballot papers in dispute were ballot papers where voters had continued a numerical sequence from their Dáil ballot paper to their European ballot paper.

- That the President of the High Court adjourned the hearing of the petition to examine the disputed ballot papers in order to ascertain whether, if admitted, they would affect the outcome of the election.

- That having conducted an examination and 'count' of the disputed ballot papers, the court determined that, even if for the purpose of that examination the court accepted the petitioner's view as to which ballot papers should be admitted, the result would not have reversed the order of the candidate on the last count. (In fact, the gap in favour of Fitzsimons would have been greater).

- That consequently, the court held that even if the returning officer had been wrong in determining which votes were invalid – and the court did not hold that she was – it would not materially affect the result and so the petition could not succeed.

Edward Byrne v William Allen, Carrie Acheson, Thomas Ambrose, Brendan Cronin, John Kennedy, Thomas Norris, The Attorney General and the Director of Public Prosecutions

Circuit Court, (Tipperary) 23 April 1980   *Sheridan J*

Reported: [1979] ILRM 282

The case arose from a petition relating to the results of the Clonmel Corporation election of June 1979. The petition was heard in October 1979, and judgment was reserved. William Allen and the Attorney General were the only respondents at this stage. On resumption to hear the judgment in November, an application was made by the other respondents to be joined to the proceedings, and it was contended that that the entire proceedings were avoided by reason of the failure to serve the Director of Public Prosecutions (DPP) with the petition in the first instance.

The court granted liberty to the additional respondents to be heard, and ordered a re-hearing of the petition afresh, as these respondents had not been present at the first hearing. The court also held that that the failure to serve the DPP did not avoid the proceedings.

The result of the last count in the election led to a tie between the petitioner Edward Byrne and the sixth-named respondent Thomas Norris on the basis that he had a higher first preference vote. There was no pause between the declaration by the returning officer of the last count and the result of the election. A person who was not the official agent of the petitioner attempted to request a re-count on behalf of the petitioner.

The Circuit Court, in ordering a re-count, held *inter alia*:

- That the returning officer should have anticipated a re-count and there should have been a considerable pause allowed between the announcement of the last count and the declaration of the final election result.

- That such a pause would have enabled the parties to digest this announcement and to make clear to him their requirements.

- That the failure to give the unsuccessful candidate or his agent the opportunity to request a re-count amounted to a denial of natural justice.

- That the relevant regulation (Local Election Regulations 1965) allowed the appointment of informal agents and the person who had applied for the recount was at least an informal agent and so her request had the same effect as if delivered by the petitioner or his officially appointed agent.

- That in a petition, there is an onus on the petitioner to show that an irregularity had occurred and that the irregularity was likely to have affected the result. In this case, the election could not have been closer, the action of the returning officer in relation to the last count was an irregularity so this onus had been discharged.

Anthony Coughlan v The Broadcasting Complaints Commission and Radio Telefís Éireann

High Court, 24 April 1998   *Carney J.*

Supreme Court 26, January 2000   *Hamilton CJ Presiding*

In the course of the 1995 divorce referendum campaign RTÉ permitted each of the political parties, all of which were in favour of a yes vote, to permit a party political broadcast during the campaign and also permitted one non-party group in favour of the yes vote and one advocating a no vote to transmit similar broadcasts.

The applicant, Mr Coughlan, complained to the Broadcasting Complaints Commission *inter alia* that RTÉ had infringed Section 18 of the Broadcasting Act 1960 as amended by the Broadcasting Authority Act 1976 that required RTÉ to be objective and impartial in all news and current affairs broadcasts. The commission rejected Mr Coughlan's complaint.

Mr Coughlan then applied to the High Court for an order that would *inter alia* quash the decision of the Broadcasting Complaints Commissions.

The High Court, in finding for Mr Coughlan, held that:

- RTÉ is free in relation to any referendum to choose to broadcast or not to broadcast any party political broadcasts or uncontested referendum broadcasts.

- A package of uncontested or partisan broadcasts by RTÉ weighted on one side of the argument is an interference with the referendum process of a kind contemplated by the Supreme Court in *McKenna v An Taoiseach* as undemocratic and is a constitutionally unfair procedure.

- On the evidence presented, RTÉ did not appreciate sufficiently that constitutional referenda involve direct legislation by the people outside the normal representative process. RTÉ did not sufficiently appreciate that, from the standpoint of the Constitution and the laws, political parties are not *de jure* involved in the referendum process.

- RTÉ's approach had resulted in inequality amounting to unconstitutional unfairness, which would not have arisen had their starting point been to afford equality to each side of the argument to which there could only be a yes and no answer.

- In relation to broadcasting decisions, RTÉ has greater expertise than the High Court and should not be lightly interfered with. (*Brandon Book Publishers Ltd v RTÉ* [1993] ILRM 806 applied.)

RTÉ and the complaints commission, supported by the Attorney General, appealed that finding to the supreme Court, which by a majority of four to one, upheld the decision of the High Court saying inter alia.

- It was "beyond argument" that the unequal allocation of 40 minutes of uncontested time to the Yes side and just 10 minutes to the No campaign gave an advantage to the Yes side in the divorce poll.

- It was soley the prerogative of the people to amend the Constitution. Any constitutional amendment must be in accordance with the constitutional process and no interference with that process could be permitted.

- RTÉ was obliged to ensure that news and current affairs were reported and presented in an objective manner. It was under no obligation to transmit party political broadcasts, but was entitled to do so. If it did, it must have regard to fiar procedures and the Constitution. In referenda, fair procedures required "that the scales should be held equallt between those for and against the amendment".

Andrew Dillon v Minister for Post and Telegraphs and Others

High Court   *Ellis J*
Supreme Court, 3 June 1981

The plaintiff was a candidate in the Dublin North Central Constituency in the 1981 Dáil election. As such, he was entitled to send one postal communication free-of-charge to each elector in the constituency. The law then provided, as it does now, that the communication must be 'relating to the election'. In a draft of his postal communication for advance clearance to the Department of Post and Telegraphs, which then had responsibility for the postal service, the plaintiff's communication included the words "To-days politicians are dishonest because they are being political and must please the largest number of people". The department objected to the sentence and insisted that it be deleted.

The plaintiff sought *inter alia* an injunction requiring the department to accept and distribute his postal communication with this sentence included.

The High Court in refusing the relief held *inter alia* that:

- The word dishonest when applied particularly to politicians at election time associated   politicians in the mind of any fair-minded person with possible corruption, cheating, deceit   or lack of fair dealing and many other possible forms of wrongdoing, many of which would or could be offences under the criminal law and warrant prosecution and sentence.

- It was difficult to think of a word more likely to be of gross offence than the allegation of dishonesty about politicians and the department was correct in refusing the plaintiff free postage in the circumstances.

The plaintiff appealed to the Supreme Court, which, overturning the High Court verdict and granting the plaintiff the relief sought, held that:

- Politicians would not feel greatly offended by the expression of an opinion that they were dishonest and even though such a charge might be thought by some as cynical it is no more than the small coinage of the currency of political controversy.

- A charge of dishonesty is one "that rarely penetrates the epidermis of any seasoned politician".

In the matter of the election for the Dáil Éireann constituency of East Mayo held on 28 February 1973.

Thomas Dillon-Leetch v Sean Calleary, Sean Flanagan, Martin Finn,

Bernard Daly Martin Fahy.

High Court, **4 May 1973**   *Butler J (Presiding)*
Supreme Court, *31 July 1974*

The petitioner sought to have the election in the constituency of East Mayo declared void and/or to have a complete re-examination and re-count of the parcels of ballot papers on the grounds that:

(i)   The poll was conducted in an improper way in a number of polling stations;

(ii) The ballot papers were dealt with in an improper manner;

(iii) The re-count had been conducted in an improper manner.

In rejecting the petition, the High Court held *inter alia*:

- That although there was an insufficient number of polling booths in a small number of stations, other arrangements adopted meant that voters were able to vote with reasonable convenience and were adequately screened from observation.

- That the returning officer had erred in hiring two young polling clerks (one 12 years old, the other 15 years old). However, on the evidence, there was no complaint relating to the conduct of either of these polling clerks.

- That there was nothing improper in party agents collecting polling cards from voters. Voters' cards have no significance or purpose except to inform the voter of his number and the place at which he is entitled to vote, and the voter is free to retain it or give it to whoever he wants.

- That the returning officer had erred in leaving the ballot papers overnight unsealed at the count centre after the first day of the count and before the re-count on the second day. However, the ballot papers were at all times under Garda observation and protection, and agents from all parties had been invited to stay in the count centre. However, an absolute duty is placed on the returning officer during such periods to place the ballot boxes and ballot papers under his own seal, and the returning officer failed to fulfil this duty.

- That the court was satisfied that, during the periods when the returning officer was absent, the ballot papers were properly guarded and that no one saw, touched or interfered with them. On the evidence, the principles of secrecy of the ballot and freedom from interference had been upheld, and the failure by the returning officer to comply with the rules as to the sealing of the papers should not be allowed to interfere with the wishes of the electorate properly expressed.

- That the re-count had been properly conducted. The rules speak not of a re-examination and re-count of ballot papers but of parcels of ballot papers. This court held that this could only refer to the parcels as they exist at the time when the request for the re-count is granted. On grounds of reasonableness, it cannot be construed as requiring the identification and checking the accuracy of intermediate transfers, which have become scattered, maybe at more than one remove among the ballot papers.

- The court commented that the resort to the procedure of an election petition in this instance was an excessive means of drawing attention to such complaints as the petitioner may have had that a more thorough appreciation of the rules and practice of elections might have avoided some of his complaints altogether.

In upholding the High Court decision on appeal, the Supreme Court held:

- That the Supreme Court had a constitutional appellate jurisdiction in respect of a Dáil election petition.

Nora Draper v The Attorney General and Others

High Court, 28 February 1983   *McMahon J*
Supreme Court, 10 February 1984   *O'Higgins CJ, Walsh,*
                                                                    Henchy, Griffin and
                                                                    McCarthy JJ

Reported: [1984] IR 277

The plaintiff suffered from multiple sclerosis and because of her chronic physical disability was unable to go to cast her vote at Dáil elections. The plaintiff challenged several provisions of the electoral acts (then in force) and sought a declaration that she as a citizen of Ireland was entitled to be provided with facilities to cast her vote.

The plaintiff was unsuccessful in the High Court. The Supreme Court, disallowing her appeal, held:

- That whereas the right to vote is a right to be exercised personally, it is not one of the personal rights of citizens dealt with in the Constitution under the heading of fundamental rights.

- That the right to vote in Dáil elections granted to citizens by virtue of Article 16, unlike other rights, is not conferred because of citizenship alone. It is only conferred on citizens who reach the prescribed age and who comply with the provisions of the law relating to the election of members of the Dáil and who are not disqualified by law from voting.
- That the statute (then in place) provided a reasonable regulation of such elections, having regard to the obligation of secrecy, the need to prevent abuses and other requirements of the common good. The fact that some voters are unable to comply with its provisions does not of itself oblige the State to tailor that law to suit special needs.

- That the State may well regard the cost and risk involved in providing facilities for particular groups as not justified, having regard to the numbers involved, their wide dispersal throughout the country, the risks of electoral abuses.

- That the State could, because of the plaintiff's incapacity, have made particular provisions for the exercise by her of her voting rights. The fact that the State did not do so did not necessarily mean that the provisions which were made were necessarily unreasonable, unjust or arbitrary or constituted a breach of the plaintiff's constitutional right to equality under Article 40.1.

- That the failure by the State to provide facilities for the plaintiff to vote did not amount to interference by the State in the exercise of the plaintiff's constitutional right to vote, nor did it amount to a breach of the constitutional obligation to ensure equality of citizens before the law.

Patrick Graham v Ireland and the Attorney General, Minister for the Environment, Brid Gavin and Proinsias B O'Guidhra

High Court, 1 May 1996,   *Morris J*

This case arose from an incident that took place at a polling station during the general election of February 1987. The plaintiff sued for defamation and negligence arising out of the fact that he was not permitted to cast his vote when he arrived at Ballybrown national school at Corcamore, County Limerick. The second-named defendant Ms Gavin was presiding officer at the polling station in question, and it was she who refused to allow him to vote.

At the hearing of the action, when the plaintiff had finished putting his case, Morris J directed that the case be withdrawn from the jury on the grounds that the refusal to allow him to vote and the words used in so doing were not capable of defamatory meaning.

The High Court considered whether the defendant was denied of his right to vote by reason of the negligence of the defendants and, in particular, the presiding officer Ms Gavin. The court held *inter alia*:

- That as a finding of fact, the plaintiff's name was on the register at no. 652 as 'Graham, Patrick Jnr,' and he was properly entitled to vote at the station on the polling day in question.

- That on the evidence Ms Gavin, as presiding officer, had earlier that day in error issued a ballot paper to the plaintiff's father who was also called Patrick in respect of the name Patrick Graham Jnr at no. 652 on the register. Notwithstanding the fact that Ms Gavin knew both the plaintiff and his father and was remotely connected with them through marriage, she had valid grounds for reaching the decision that the name at no. 652 on the register referred to the plaintiff's father.

- That although Ms Gavin had acted in error, this act did not amount to negligence on her part and accordingly the plaintiff's claim failed.

In the matter of Article 26 of the Constitution and the Matter of the Electoral (Amendment) Bill 1961

Supreme Court, 14 July 1961   *Maguire CJ; Lavery;*
                                                        Kingsmill Moore;
Reported: [1961] IR 169   *O'Dálaigh; Haugh JJ;*

The High Court, in *O'Donovan v Attorney General* ([1961] IR 114) declared that the Electoral (Amendment) Act 1959 was in part repugnant to the Constitution. As a result, a new Act, the Electoral (Amendment) Act

1961, which *inter alia* set out a new revision of constituencies, was enacted by the Oireachtas, and under Article 26 of the Constitution, the President referred it to the Supreme Court.

The Supreme Court in holding that the bill was not repugnant to the Constitution said *inter alia*:

- That the population to be considered in fixing the total number of members of Dáil Éireann and in the revision of constituencies pursuant to Article 16 of the Constitution was the population as ascertained at the last preceding completed census.
- That exact parity in the ratio between members and the population of each constituency is unlikely to be obtained and is not required.

- That the decision as to the extent of parity (in the ratio between deputies and population) which was practicable was a matter for the Oireachtas. The courts should not review the Oireachtas decision in this regard unless there has been a manifest infringement of the provision of Article 16 of the Constitution.

- That the courts would not lay down a figure above or below which a deviation from the national average would not be permissible but would only interfere in a case where the divergence from the national average was such as to make it clear that the requirements of the Constitution had not been carried out.

In the Matter of Article 26 of the Constitution and in the Matter of the Electoral (Amendment) Act 1983.

Supreme Court, 8 February 1984   *O'Higgins CJ*

Reported: [1984] IR 268; [1984] ILRM 539

The Electoral Amendment Bill 1983 included a provision that would enable British citizens to vote in Dáil elections. A British citizen would be registered as a Dáil elector in a constituency if they were ordinarily resident in that constituency. The President, pursuant to Article 26 of the Constitution, referred the bill to the Supreme Court to determine whether the bill or any of its provisions were repugnant to the Constitution.

In holding that the bill was repugnant to the Constitution, the Supreme Court held *inter alia*:

- That in declaring that all power derives under God from the people whose right it is designated the ruler of the state and in final appeal to decide all questions of national policy the provision of Article 6 of the Constitution (with Articles 12 and Article 47) required that the right to vote at elections for members of Dáil Éireann conferred on every citizen by Article 16 of the Constitution was restricted to citizens who formed part of the island of Ireland.

- That the provision of Article 16 of the Constitution of Ireland indicates a "total code for the holding of elections to Dáil Éireann" and sets out the matters, which would appear to be necessary other than the minor regulatory provisions.

- That this code provides for the eligibility of candidates, the persons entitled to vote, limitation of one vote for each voter, the standards for determining the number of members for each constituency; a limiting time within which general elections must take place after a dissolution; the maximum term of a Dáil; a provision for the timing of polling throughout the country; and an obligation to provide for the automatic election of the Chairman of the Dáil.

- That in contrast with this essential features of elections for Dáil Éireann, the matters which are left to be regulated by law would appear to be *(a)* disqualification of citizens from voting; *(b)* provisions with which citizens must comply in order to have the right to vote; *(c)* the fixing of the number of members of Dáil Éireann within the ratio laid down by the Constitution *(d)* the provision subject to the minimum of three of the number of members for each constituency *(e)* the fixing of the date of a general election subject to a restriction as to the maximum period after the dissolution of the Dáil; *(f)* the period during which the same Dáil may continue subject to the constitutional maximum of seven years and *(g)* the details of the mandatory provision for the re-election of the Chairman of Dáil Éireann.

O'Donovan v Attorney General

High Court, 20 February 1960   **Budd J**

Reported: [1961] IR 114; [1962] 96 ILTR 121

The plaintiff sought *inter alia* a declaration that the 1959 Electoral (Amendment) Act, which sought to implement a revision of constituencies for Dáil elections was repugnant to the Constitution because the scheme of constituencies proposed by it was such as to produce a substantial departure from the requirement that as far as practical there be a parity in the ratio of the members of the Dáil to the population in each constituency.

The statistical evidence presented in the case showed that on the basis of the 1956 census of population the new constituency scheme proposed in the Act would mean that western constituencies would have significantly fewer people per deputy whereas Dublin constituencies would have more people for deputy. The most extreme contrasts was that Galway South would have a ratio of 1 deputy: 23,128 people, whereas Dublin South West would have 1 deputy :16,575.

The High Court, granting the plaintiff the relief, held *inter alia*:

- That the Constitution does not require an "all but mathematical parity of ratio" of member to population but rather a parity of ratio as far as that is capable of being carried into action in a practical way.

- That the provision does not mean that mere convenience is a justification for a divergence from parity of representation.

- That there was no constitutional justification for allowing matters, such as communication difficulties, geographical distance, the breech of county boundaries or the fact that the population Dublin might not have occasion to make such great demands on their deputies to influence the ratio of population to deputies. The working of the parliamentary system itself is not relevant in this regard.

- That in enacting the Electoral (Amendment) Act 1959, the legislature did not have due regard to the changes of distribution of the population set out in the 1956 census and therefore the Act was repugnant to Article 16 of the Constitution.

Sean D Loftus and Others v The Attorney General, John Kenny and Liam O'Buachalla.

Supreme Court, 11 May 1978   *O'Higgins CJ; Finlay P;*

Reported: [1979] IR 221   *Henchy, Parke, Hamilton JJ*

The defendants had applied in 1965 to the Clerk of the Dáil in his capacity as Registrar of Political Parties to have their party registered in the register of political parties, which *inter alia* would enable the name of the party to be inserted under their candidates' names on the ballot paper.

The Registrar rejected their application. They appealed to the Appeal Board provided for this purpose by the legislation. The Appeal Board consisted of a judge of the High Court, the Ceann Comhairle of Dáil Éireann and the Cathaoirleach of the Seanad. The Appeal Board, in a decision delivered on 19 March 1965, upheld the Registrar's decision to reject their application.

The plaintiff then applied (with some tardiness after the initial filing of application) to the High Court for various declarations.

The High Court held that:

- The Appeal Board was not properly constituted on 19 March 1965 since it had met after the Dáil had been dissolved but before the new Dáil was elected and therefore the Ceann Comhairle was not in office at the time and consequently its decision was invalid.

On appeal to the Supreme Court by the plaintiffs and the second-named defendant (who had been chairman of the Appeal Board).

The Supreme Court, in disallowing the plaintiff's appeal but allowing the second defendant's appeal, held:

- That the power to register political parties conferred on the Registrar by the Act was not an arbitrary power, nor did it contravene Article 15, subsection 2, of the Constitution.

- That the right to have a political party included on the register is not a personal right within the meaning of Article 40 of the Constitution.

- That the provision of the legislation enabling the name of a candidate's political party to appear on his nomination paper and on ballot papers did not constitute an infringement of the citizen's right to free association guaranteed by Article 40.6.i of the Constitution

- That the duties and functions of the Ceann Comhairle may be discharged and performed by him in the interval between the dissolution of one Dáil and the Election of the Ceann Comhairle of the next Dáil. Accordingly, the Appeal Board as it met on 19 March 1965 had been properly constituted.

- That in deciding whether an applicant party was a 'genuine political party' within the meaning of the Act, the Registrar of Political

Parties should ascertain whether the applicant party is bound together by the cohesion of common political beliefs and by its being organised for electoral purposes into an entity to such an extent and with such distinctiveness as to justify its claim to be a political party.

• That the words 'organised to contest a Dáil Election' in the Act refer not to the degree or perfection of the existing organisation of the applicant party but to the fact of its being organised for that object and purpose.

• That the provisions of the Act that enable the registering of a political party which seeks to operate in one particular area do not refer to political parties that have or claim a national aim or objective but which, by reason of their weakness, are restricted to activity in on particular area

Roy Murphy v Independent Radio and Television Commission and the Attorney General.

High Court, 25 April 1997   *Geoghegan J*
Supreme Court, 28 May 1998   *Hamilton CJ, O' Flaherty, Denham,*
                                                       Barrington and Keane JJ
Reported: [1998] 2 ILRM 362

The plaintiff, who was a pastor attached to the Irish Faith Centre, challenged a decision of the Independent Radio and Television Commission to refuse to permit an independent radio station (98 FM) to broadcast an advertisement about public showings of a video on the resurrection of Christ, which the Irish Faith Centre was hosting each evening for Easter week.

At issue in the case was section 10(3) of the Radio and Television Act 1988, which prohibits the broadcast of any advertisement that is directed towards any religious or political end or that has any relation to an industrial dispute.

Although the judgment dealt with an advertisement that was religious in nature, the judgment also had a particular relevance for the prohibition on political advertising in the broadcast media.

The High Court refused the relief sought.

On appeal, the Supreme Court held *inter alia*:

- That the right to communicate is one of the most basic rights of man and is an unspecified right implied by Article 40.3 of the Constitution.

- That Article 40.6, which is concerned with the public activities of the citizen in a democratic society, guarantees the right of citizens to express freely their convictions and opinions. This involves the right not only to communicate convictions or opinions but also to communicate the facts on which they are based.

- That the prohibition on certain types of advertising constitutes a limitation on the right to communicate under the Constitution and on the right to freedom of expression under Article 40 thereof. However, these are personal rights which can be limited by the Oireachtas in the interests of the common good (*Ryan v Attorney General* [1965] IR 294 applied)

- That in regulating the exercise of constitutional rights in the interest of the common good, the limitations imposed by the Oireachtas must be proportionate with the purpose that the legislation seeks to achieve.

- That although a more selective administrative system for dealing with religious advertising, as opposed to a blanket ban, was possible, this was matter for the Oireachtas and the ban imposed respected the principle of proportionality.

- That all three types of banned advertisements relate to matters which have proved extremely divisive in the past (religion, politics, industrial disputes). The Oireachtas was entitled to take the view that citizens would resent having advertisements touching on these topics broadcast into their homes and that such advertising, if permitted, might lead to unrest.

- That the Oireachtas may well have thought that, in relation to matters of such sensitivity, rich men should not be able to buy access to the airwaves to the detriment of their poorer rivals.

- That the limitations placed on the various constitutional rights are minimal; the applicant has the right to advance his views in speech, by writing or by holding assemblies or by associating with like-minded persons. The only restriction placed on his activities is that he cannot advance his views by a paid advertisement on radio and television.

Niall McMahon v Attorney General

High Court, 11 December 1969   *Pringle J*
Supreme Court, 4 October 1970

Reported: [1972] IR 69; (1972) 106 ILTR 89

The plaintiff sought *inter alia* a declaration that the [then] provisions of the electoral acts infringed the Constitution in that they breached the requirement for secrecy of the ballot.

At that time, the electoral acts required that when a ballot paper was being issued to a voter that the serial number of the ballot paper issued be written beside that voter's name on the polling station's copy of the register of electors.

In finding for the plaintiff and making the declaration, the High Court held *inter alia*:

- That the term 'secret ballot' in the Constitution means a ballot in which there is complete and inviolable secrecy.

- That the provisions of the Act whereby the voter's number on the electoral registrar was written on the counterfoil raised the possibility that voters completed ballot paper might be identified, and this was inconsistent with the secrecy of the ballot required by the Constitution.

- That the special arrangements in the Act, whereby a blind, incapacitated or illiterate voter could be assisted to vote were instances where the particular voter has elected to waive his constitutional right to complete secrecy.

On appeal, upholding the High Court on the central issue and holding again for the plaintiff, the Supreme Court (by a 3-2 majority) held *inter alia*:

- That the secrecy of the ballot required under the Constitution was an absolute one and not a qualified one.

- That the Constitution does not require the voting citizen to run the risk of disclosure by accident or breach of the law: it entitles him to shut up within privacy of his own mind all knowledge of the manner in which he voted.

- That a voting system that permits a state official to note the number of the ballot paper of each voter in the state and, which requires this information to be stored for a full year after the poll, of itself offends against the spirit and substance of the declaration that voting shall be by secret ballot. Under such a system, the fear of disclosure, which secrecy is designed to drive away, is ostentatiously retained.

- That the special provisions for incapacitated voters were not justified on the grounds of a waiver by such electors of their right to vote in complete secrecy but were justified on that grounds that they provided a method of voting that was as secret as possible, having regard to the limits imposed by the incapacity of the elector.

Christopher O'Malley and Brid Hayes v An Taoiseach and the Attorney General

High Court 23 May 1989   *Hamilton P*

Reported: [1990] ILRM 461

The Dáil constituencies had been redrawn in 1983 by the Electoral (Amendment) Act of that year. However, in 1986, a new census had been taken, which showed substantial changes in population distribution throughout the country. The plaintiff sought, *inter alia*, an injunction to restrain the Taoiseach from advising the President to dissolve the Dáil, thereby causing an election. The plaintiff's argument was that the ratio between the number of members to be elected for each constituency and its population did not comply with the requirements of Article 16 of the Constitution.

The High Court, in refusing the application for the injunction, held:

- That on the evidence since the enactment of the Electoral Amendment Act 1983 there had been substantial changes in the distribution of the population and as a consequence thereof the ratio between the number of members to be elected for each constituency, as ascertained at the last preceding census, was not so far as practicable, the same throughout the country.

- That the constitutional obligation placed on the Oireachtas is not discharged by revising the constituencies once in every twelve years. They are obliged to revise the constituencies with due regard to changes in distribution of the population and when a census return discloses major changes in the distribution the population there is a constitutional obligation on the Oireachtas to revise the constituencies.

- That the constitutional duty of dissolving the Dáil is vested in the President, and he is not answerable to any court in the exercise and performance of his duty.

- That the constitutional duty of advising the President in relation to this question is vested in the Taoiseach, and the courts have no jurisdiction to place any impediment between them.

Patrick O' Reilly v Minister for the Environment

High Court 21 March 1986   *Murphy J*

Reported: [1986] IR 143

The plaintiff sought, *inter alia*, a declaration that the procedure provided by law that candidates' names should be listed on the ballot paper in alphabetical order infringed fairness of procedure and the constitutional right to equality.

The High Court, in dismissing the claim, held:

- That on the evidence, the alphabetical listing of candidates' names significantly favours those candidates who took alphabetical precedence and were placed higher up on the ballot paper.

- That this bias for the higher placed candidates reflected not a defect in the system itself but rather is a measure of some degree of indifference by the electorate or some of them as to how their votes – and in particular their second and subsequent preferences are cast.

- That the system of alphabetical listing poses the practical advantage – particularly in a constituency where there are a number of candidates – that the voter can quickly find any particular candidates.

- That an alphabetical listing is an established procedure in so many fields that it is seen as being a reasonable practical solution to selecting or preparing a set of names.

- That the alphabetical system of listing candidates constitutes a reasonable regulation of elections by the Oireachtas (*O'Donovan v Attorney General* [1961] IR 114 applied).

John Ormonde and Seamus Dolan v Seán Mac Gabhann and the Attorney General

High Court, 9 July 1969   *Pringle J*

Unreported

The plaintiffs wished to contest the Seanad election on the labour vocational panel. They made informal enquiries to the Clerk of the Seanad who intimated that, in his opinion, their qualifications were not sufficient to entitle them to be nominated to the labour panel. The plaintiffs applied to the High Court seeking a declaration that they were qualified to contest the election on the panel.

The first issue with which the court had to deal was whether the plaintiffs could apply to the High Court for such a ruling as the relevant legislation laid down a procedure, whereby the question of the qualification of any person for a panel is determined by the Seanad Returning Officer with a judicial assessor after the close of nominations. The legislation provides that this judicial assessor must be a judge of the High Court.

Granting the plaintiffs the relief sought, Pringle J held:

- That the procedure provided for by legislation does not deprive persons who, like the plaintiffs, have not been nominated to any panel, from having their qualifications for nomination to a particular panel decided by the High Court. If such a person's nomination for a particular panel are not considered adequate by the judicial referee, they would be too late to be nominated to any other panel for which they might be qualified.

- That the only qualification required by the Constitution and the Act are that the person has knowledge and practical experience in the interest or in the service of labour whether organised or unorganised. The Constitution does not say that they must have special knowledge and practical experience, nor does it indicate that they must have acquired this knowledge and expertise in any particular manner.

- That mere membership of a trade union would not of itself be sufficient to qualify one for nomination to the labour panel.

- That on the evidence, the plaintiffs who had both been officers in local trade union branches, members of Dáil Éireann and had previously been elected to the Seanad on the labour panel were deemed to have the required knowledge and experience of labour issues to qualify them to be nominated on the labour panel.

Carl Quinn, Orla Walsh, Maria Quaid, Michael Fox, Siobhan Doyle, Simon Nolan and Albert Heffernan v The Lord Mayor, Alderman and Burgess of the City of Waterford.

Supreme Court, 27 November 1990   *Finlay CJ, Hederman J,*

Reported: [1990] 2 IR 507   *McCarthy J*

The plaintiffs were students at Waterford Regional Technical College, all of whose family homes were outside the county of Waterford. They were all on the register of electors in their home constituencies. When they applied to be registered in the city of Waterford, the county registrar rejected their application as they were all registered in other constituencies and were not entitled to be registered more than once.

The students appealed the county registrar's decision to the Circuit Court, and their appeal was disallowed by Judge Sheridan. They appealed the Circuit Court's decision to the Supreme Court on a point of law.

The Supreme Court, in granting the appeal and ordering the county registrar to reconsider their application to be placed on the register of electors, held:

- That a person could be 'ordinarily registered' in more than one place within the meaning of the Act.

- That the appellants were ordinarily resident in Waterford during the academic year.

- That the constitutional ban is on double voting not on double registering. Although the Constitution provided that no voter may exercise more than on vote at an election, there was no legislative prohibition on double registration as a means of enforcing the constitutional prohibition on double voting.

- That the right of the county registrar to make enquiries of someone applying to be registered as to whether they were already on the register of electors was limited to enquiries concerning the applicant's condition or status in that constituency, and he could not make enquiries as to whether the applicant was registered in any other constituency.

Fionnuala Sherwin v Minister for the Environment, Ireland and the Attorney General

High Court, 11 March 1997   *Costello J*

The applicant sought *inter alia* a declaration that certain provisions of the legislation governing referenda then in place (the Referendum Act 1994), which enabled only members of the Oireachtas to appoint personation agents and agents at the counting of votes in referenda, were unconstitutional.

The plaintiff claimed that these provisions were unconstitutional in the circumstances of the Referendum on the Fifteenth Amendment of the Constitution ('The Divorce referendum') since all of the political parties represented in the Oireachtas supported the proposed amendment. Ad hoc groups established to campaign against the amendment, including the one of which the plaintiff was a member, did not have access through association in a political party to Oireachtas members who could nominate personation and count agents.

Under the Act, the Minister for the Environment was empowered in circumstances where a "special difficulty occurs to make special arrangements". The plaintiff had written to the Minister for the Environment during the campaign claiming that the circumstances surrounding the referendum constituted circumstances of 'special difficulty' within the meaning of the Act and urged the Minister to invoke his powers under the act to make special arrangements. The Minister had replied to her saying that he had no power to amend the statutory requirement that only Oireachtas members could appointed election agents.

In refusing the plaintiff the declaration sought, the High Court held:

- That the power conferred on the Minister to make special arrangements is a discretionary one. It may be exercised only in the circumstances specified in the section, namely where there is an emergency or special difficulty.

- That the power conferred is to make such adaptation or modification of any statute, order or regulation referred to in the section. If, in the Minster's opinion, it is necessary to enable referenda to be duly held, he may make an order under the section, but it must comply with the 'principles' of the Acts dealing with referenda.

- That if the Minister had been satisfied that a 'special difficulty' had arisen in relation to the holding of the referendum, he has the power to modify the legislation insofar as would have been necessary to enable personation agents to be appointed by means other than exclusively by Oireachtas members.

- That the statutory mechanism for dealing with 'special difficulties' by ministerial order served to remedy any possible constitutional invalidity of the section enabling only Oireachtas members to appoint polling and count agents.

- *Obiter*: That personation agents are appointed not for the purposes of enabling political parties or groups of persons associated with campaigns in referenda to detect or deter personation by their political opponents but are appointed to assist returning officers in ensuring compliance with the laws against personation. Similarly, agents at the count are appointed to help the returning officer count the votes properly – not to detect possible malpractice by political opponents.

The plaintiff had also argued that because the count was not held in public and open to all members of the public to attend the section was unconstitutional. The court held:

- That the Constitution permits the Oireachtas to regulate the manner in which referenda are held and there were obvious practical reasons why access to the count should be limited in this fashion. He held there could be no possible objection to doing so.

The issue raised by the plaintiff's complaint was subsequently redressed by a provision of the Referendum Act 1997, which provides that, in addition to personation agents being appointed by Oireachtas members, other groups can apply to the Referendum Commission to be allowed to appoint such agents.

In the matter of Bunreacht na hÉireann, Patricia McKenna v An Taoiseach and Others

High Court, 31 October 1995   *Keane J*
Supreme Court, 17 November 1995

Reported: [1995] 2 IR 10.

The case arose from the decision of Dáil Éireann to vote £500,000 to the Minister for Equality and Law Reform to be used for a publicity and advertising campaign to encourage a yes vote in the referendum on the Fifteenth Amendment to the Constitution Bill (the "divorce referendum").

The plaintiff argued that the use of public funds by the government to promote a particular outcome in the referendum infringed the procedure laid down for the conduct of referenda by Article 46 and Article 47 of the Constitution and that it infringed her constitutional personal rights as a citizen.

The plaintiff failed in the High Court, which held *inter alia*:

- That the plaintiff had *locus standi* to institute and maintain the proceedings;

- That Articles 17 and 28 of the Constitution entrusts the power to raise and expend public moneys is exclusively to the Government and the Dáil. For the courts to review a decision in this area would amount to a breach of the separation of powers, and it would be for the courts to assume a role, which was exclusively entrusted to the government and the Oireachtas.

The plaintiff succeeded on her appeal to the Supreme Court, which held by a 4-1 majority:

- That the government, in spending public money in support of one particular outcome, was acting in breach of the Constitution.

- That such expenditure amounted to a breach of the constitutional right to equality and had the effect of putting the voting rights of those citizens in favour of the constitutional amendments above the voting right of those opposed to it.

- That such expenditure also amounted to an infringement of the constitutional right to freedom of expression and the constitutional right to a democratic process in referenda. (Denham J)

- That the government had a right and a duty to spend money to give information to the public about the implications of a constitutional amendment, to clarify the situation and to give an explanation regarding the referendum.

- That the government could campaign for a yes vote by methods other than the expenditure of public monies and that the prohibition on the use of public funds did not mean that ministers were not entitled to use their state transport in relation to the referendum or to avail of the media to put forward their views.

In the Matter of the Fifteenth Amendment of the Constitution (No.2) Bill and in the Matter of a Referendum Petition pursuant to s.42 of the Referendum Act 1994.

Desmond Hanafin v Minister for the Environment, the Government of Ireland, the Attorney General and the Referendum Returning Officer and the Director of Public Prosecutions (Notice party).

High Court, 1996   *Murphy J,*
Supreme Court, 12 June 1996   *Hamilton CJ, O'Flaherty,*
Blayney, Denham and Barrington JJ

The case involved the petitioning of the result of the 1996 divorce referendum mainly on the grounds that the government had spent public monies in a publicity and advertising campaign urging a yes vote in favour of passing of the amendment. The Supreme Court had held in the middle of that referendum campaign in *McKenna v An Taoiseach (No.2)* 1995 2 IR 10 that spending money in this way was unconstitutional and infringed the concept of equality of all citizens. Although the government ceased spending public money on its publicity campaign for a yes vote when the Supreme Court judgment in McKenna was announced, a considerable sum had already been spent.

The referendum was held on 24 November and counting began on 25 November. After the finalisation of the count, including a full re-count, the referendum returning officer prepared the provisional referendum certificate, which recorded that 818,842 votes had been cast in favour of the amendment and 809,728 had been cast against.

The petitioner, Mr Hanafin was granted leave under section 42 of the 1994 Act to present a petition claiming the referendum was null and void on the basis that the result of the referendum as a whole was affected materially by an obstruction and/or interference with the conduct of the referendum and/or by an irregularity in the conduct of the poll.

Over the course of the trial of the petition in the High Court, the petitioner adduced evidence from various experts with regard to opinion polls, the factors influencing voting patterns, advertising and the intentions of the electorate. At the end of the presentation of the petitioner's case, the respondent sought a direction from the court that the petitioner had failed to establish his case.

The divisional court of the High Court held unanimously:

- That the campaign carried out by the government with public funds did not materially affect the result of the referendum.

- That it had not been established, in the evidence adduced by the petitioner, even as a matter of reasonable certainty that the campaign unconstitutionally funded had any ascertainable or measurable influence on the electorate when they cast their votes.

By a margin of 2-1 (Barr J dissenting) the High Court held:

- That the phrase 'conduct of the referendum' in the Act did not cover an advertising or political campaign which was intended to influence the outcome of the referendum.

On appeal, the Supreme Court dismissed the petitioner appeal holding:

- That the standard of proof which lies on the petitioner in such cases is to establish his case on the balance of probabilities.

- That the jurisdiction of the High Court in hearing a petition is not confined to the obstruction, interference or irregularity in the conduct of the poll. The phrase 'conduct of the referendum' was not to be interpreted narrowly so as to limit it to administrative procedure or the practical or physical aspects of taking a poll. It also covered unlawful and unconstitutional conduct in the referendum campaign, which materially affects the result of the referendum.

- That the Act makes it clear that regardless of the nature or extent of the wrongdoing, the result of the referendum cannot be impugned with or interfered with by a petition if the result of the referendum as a whole was not materially affected by such wrong doing. The onus to prove that the result was materially affected by the wrong-doing lies on the petitioner.

- That the spending of public monies by the government on the campaign for a Yes vote was unconstitutional and was an interference in the conduct of the referendum

- That there was no basis upon which the Supreme Court could interfere with the divisional court's finding of fact that the government advertising campaign for an affirmative vote had not materially affected the result of the referendum.

Redmond v Minister for the Environment, Ireland and the Attorney General

High Court, June 1997   *Shanley J*, ex tempore

The plaintiff has sought to be a candidate in the previous general election in the Wexford constituency. However, the returning officer had declined to accept the plaintiff's nomination paper because he refused to lodge the necessary deposit.

A few days after a new general election had been called in June 1997, the plaintiff sought an injunction to restrain the holding of the general election in the Wexford constituency on the grounds that the deposit requirement was repugnant to the constitutional provisions regarding the conduct of Dáil elections (Article 16) and the equality provisions of the Constitution. (Article 40)

The High Court, refusing the plaintiff the injunction sought, in an *ex tempore* judgment, held:

That although the plaintiff might have a statable case, he had not made his application in adequate time, and there was now a greater public interest in allowing the impending general election to proceed.

Appendix 2

Constitutional Provisions
on Elections and Referenda

1. POPULAR DEMOCRACY

Article 6.1
All powers of government, legislative, executive and judicial, derive, under God, from the people, whose right it is to designate the rulers of the State and, in final appeal, to decide all questions of national policy, according to the requirements of the common good.

Article 6.2
These powers of government are exercisable only by or on the authority of the organs of State established by this Constitution.

2. THE PRESIDENCY AND PRESIDENTIAL ELECTIONS

Article 12.1
There shall be a President of Ireland (*Uachtarán na hÉireann*), hereinafter called the President, who shall take precedence over all other persons in the State and who shall exercise and perform the powers and functions conferred on the President by this Constitution and by law.

Article 12.2.1°
The President shall be elected by direct vote of the people.

Article 12.2.2°
Every citizen who has the right to vote at an election for members of Dáil Éireann shall have the right to vote at an election for President.

Article 12.2.2°
The voting shall be by secret ballot and on the system of proportional representation by means of the single transferable vote.

Article 12.3.1°
The President shall hold office for seven years from the date upon which he enters upon his office, unless before the expiration of that period he dies, or resigns, or is removed from office, or becomes permanently incapacitated, such incapacity being established to the satisfaction of the Supreme Court consisting of not less than five judges.

Article 12.3.2°
A person who holds or who has held, office as President, shall be eligible for re-election to that office once, but only once.

Article 12.3.3°
An election for the office of President shall be held not later than, and not earlier than the sixtieth day before, the date of the expiration of the term of office of every President, but in the event of the removal from office of the President or of his death, resignation, or permanent incapacity established as aforesaid (whether occurring before or after he enters upon his office), an election for the office of President shall be held within sixty days after such event.

Article 12.4.1°
Every citizen who has reached his thirty-fifth year of age is eligible for election to the office of President.

Article 12.4.2°
Every candidate for election, not a former or retiring President, must be nominated either by:

    i. not less than twenty persons, each of whom is at the time a member of one of the Houses of the oireachtas or

    ii. by the Councils of not less than four administrative Counties (including County Boroughs) as defined by law.

Article 12.4.3°
No person and no such Council shall be entitled to subscribe to the nomination of more than one candidate in respect of the same election.

Article 12.4.4°
Former or retiring Presidents may become candidates on their own nomination.

Article 12.4.5°
Where only one candidate is nominated for the office of President it shall not be necessary to proceed to a ballot for his election.

Article 12.5
Subject to the provisions of this Article, elections for the office of President shall be regulated by law.

Article 12.6.1°
The President shall not be a member of either House of the Oireachtas.

Article 12.6.2°
If a member of either House of the Oireachtas be elected President, he shall be deemed to have vacated his seat in that House.

Article 12.6.3°
The President shall not hold any other office or position of emolument.

Article 12.7
The first President shall enter upon his office as soon as may be after his election, and every subsequent President shall enter upon his office on the day following the expiration of the term of office of his predecessor or as soon as may be thereafter or, in the event of his predecessor's removal from office, death, resignation, or permanent incapacity established as provided by section 3 hereof, as soon as may be after the election.

3. THE DÁIL AND DÁIL ELECTIONS

Article 15.14
No person may be at the same time a member of both Houses of the Oireachtas, and, if any person who is already a member of either House becomes a member of the other House, he shall forthwith be deemed to have vacated his first seat.

Article 16.1.1°
Every citizen without distinction of sex who has reached the age of twenty-one years, and who is not placed under disability or incapacity by this Constitution or by law, shall be eligible for membership of Dáil Éireann.

Article 16.1.2°
   i.   All citizens, and

ii. such other persons in the State as may be determined by law, without distinction of sex who have reached the age of eighteen years who are not disqualified by law and comply with the provisions of the law relating to the election of members of Dáil Éireann, shall have the right to vote at an election for members of Dáil Éireann.

Article 16.1.3°
No law shall be enacted placing any citizen under disability or incapacity for membership of Dáil Éireann on the ground of sex or disqualifying any citizen or other person from voting at an election for members of Dáil Éireann on that ground.

Article 16.1.4°
No voter may exercise more than one vote at an election for Dáil Éireann, and the voting shall be by secret ballot.

Article 16.2.1°
Dáil Éireann shall be composed of members who represent constituencies determined by law.

Article 16.2.2°
The number of members shall from time to time be fixed by law, but the total number of members of Dáil Éireann shall not be fixed at less than one member for each thirty thousand of the population, or at more than one member for each twenty thousand of the population.

Article 16.2.3°
The ratio between the number of members to be elected at any time for each constituency and the population of each constituency, as ascertained at the last preceding census, shall, so far as it is practicable, be the same throughout the country.

Article 16.2.4°
The Oireachtas shall revise the constituencies at least once in every twelve years, with due regard to changes in distribution of the population, but any alterations in the constituencies shall not take effect during the life of Dáil Éireann sitting when such revision is made.

Articles 16.2.5°
The members shall be elected on the system of proportional representation by means of the single transferable vote.

Articles 16.2.6°
No law shall be enacted whereby the number of members to be returned for any constituency shall be less than three.

Article 16.3.1°
Dáil Éireann shall be summoned and dissolved as provided by section 2 of Article 2 of this Constitution.

Article 16.3.2°
A general election for members of Dáil Éireann shall take place not later than thirty days after dissolution of Dáil Éireann.

Article 16.4.1°
Polling at every general election for Dáil Éireann shall as far as practicable take place on the same day throughout the country.

Article 16.4.2°
Dáil Éireann shall meet within thirty days from that polling day.

Article 16.5
The same Dáil Éireann shall not continue for a longer period than seven years from the date of its first meeting: a shorter period may be fixed by law.

Article 16.6
Provision shall be made by law to enable the member of Dáil Éireann who is the Chairman immediately before dissolution of Dáil Éireann to be deemed without any actual election to be elected a member of Dáil Éireann at the ensuing general election.

Article 16.7
Subject to the foregoing provisions of this Article, elections for membership of Dáil Éireann, including the filling of casual vacancies, shall be regulated in accordance with law.

4. THE SEANAD AND SEANAD ELECTIONS

Article 18.1
Seanad Éireann shall be composed of sixty members, of whom eleven shall be nominated members and forty-nine shall be elected members.

Article 18.2
A person to be eligible for membership of Seanad Éireann must be eligible to become a member of Dáil Éireann.

Article 18.3
The nominated members of Seanad Éireann shall be nominated, with their prior consent, by the Taoiseach who is appointed next after the reassembly of Dáil Éireann following the dissolution thereof which occasions the nomination of the said members.

Article 18.4.1°
The elected members of Seanad Éireann shall be elected as follows:

i. Three shall be elected by the National University of Ireland.

ii. Three shall be elected by the University of Dublin.

iii. Forty-three shall be elected from panels of candidates constituted as hereinafter provided.

Article 18.4.2°
Provision may be made by law for the election, on a franchise and in the manner to be provided by law, by one or more of the following institutions, namely:

i. The universities mentioned in subsection 1 of this section,

ii. Any other institutions of higher education in the State,

of so many members of Seanad Éireann as may be fixed by law in substitution for an equal number of the members to be elected pursuant to paragraphs i and ii of the said subsection 1.

A member or members of Seanad Éireann may be elected under this subsection by institutions grouped together or by a single institution.

Article 18.4.3°
Nothing in this Article shall be invoked to prohibit the dissolution by law of a university mentioned in subsection 1 of this section.

Article 18.5
Every election of the elected members of Seanad Éireann shall be held on

the system of proportional representation by means of the single transferable vote, and by secret postal ballot.

Article 18.6
The members of Seanad Éireann to be elected by the Universities shall be elected on a franchise and in the manner to be provided by law.

Article 18.7.1°
Before each general election of the members of Seanad Éireann to be elected from panels of candidates, five panels of candidates shall be formed in the manner provided by law containing respectively the names of persons having knowledge and practical experience of the following interests and services, namely:

 i.   National Language and Culture, Literature, Art, Education and such professional interests as may be defined by law for the purpose of this panel;

 ii. Agriculture and allied interests and Fisheries;

 iii. Labour, whether organised or unorganised;

 iv. Industry and Commerce, including banking, finance, accountancy, engineering and architecture;

 v.   Public Administration and social services, including voluntary social activities.

Article 18.7.2°
Not more than eleven and, subject to the provisions of Article 19 hereof, less than five members of Seanad Éireann shall be elected from any one panel.

Article 18.8
A general election for Seanad Éireann shall take place not later than ninety days after dissolution of Dáil Éireann, and the first meeting of Seanad Éireann after the general election shall take place on a day to be fixed by the President on the advice of the Taoiseach.

Article 18.9
Every member of Seanad Éireann shall, unless he previously dies, resigns,

or becomes disqualified, continue to hold office until the day before the polling day of the general election for Seanad Éireann next held after his election or nomination.

Article 18.10.1°
Subject to the foregoing provisions of this Article elections of the elected members of Seanad Éireann shall be regulated by law.

Article 18.10.2°
Casual vacancies in the number of the nominated members of Seanad Éireann shall be filled by nomination by the Taoiseach with the prior consent of persons so nominated.

Article 18.10.3°
Casual vacancies in the number of the elected members of Seanad Éireann shall be filled in the manner provided by law.

Article 19
Provision may be made by law for the direct election by any functional or vocational group or association or council of so many members of Seanad Éireann as may be fixed by such law in substitution for an equal number of the members to be elected from the corresponding panels of candidates constituted under Article 18 of this Constitution.

5. LOCAL GOVERNMENT AND LOCAL ELECTIONS

Article 28 A
1. The State recognises the role of Local Government in providing a forum for the democratic representation of local communities, in exercising and performing at local level powers and functions conferred by law and in promoting by its initiatives the interest of such communities.

2. There shall be such directly elected local authorities as may be determined by law and their powers and functions shall be subject to the provisions of this constitution, be so determined and shall be exercised and performed in accordance with law.

3. Elections for members of such local authorities shall be held in accordance with law not later than the end of the fifth year after the year in which they were last held.

4. Every citizen who has a right to vote at an election for members of Dáil Eireann and such other person as may be determined by law shall have the right to vote at an election for members of such of the local authorities referred to in section 2 of this article as shall be determined by law.

5. Casual vacancies in the membership of local authorities shall be filled in accordance with law.

6. PROHIBITION ON COMPTROLLER AND AUDITOR GENERAL BEING A MEMBER OF THE OIREACHTAS

Article 33.3
The Comptroller and Auditor General shall not be a member of either House of the Oireachtas and shall not hold any other office or position of emolument.

7. PROHIBITIONS ON MEMBERS OF THE JUDICIARY BEING MEMBERS OF THE OIREACHTAS

Article 35.3
No judge shall be eligible to be a member of either House of the Oireachtas or to hold any other office or position of emolument.

8. AMENDMENT OF THE CONSTITUTION AND REFERENDA

Article 46.1
Any provision of this Constitution may be amended, whether by way of variation, addition, or repeal, in the manner provided by this Article.

Article 46.2
Every proposal for an amendment of this Constitution shall be initiated in Dáil Éireann as a Bill, and shall upon having been passed or deemed to have been passed by both Houses of the Oireachtas, be submitted by Referendum to the decision of the people in accordance with the law for the time being in force relating to the Referendum.

Article 46.3
Every such Bill shall be expressed to be "An Act to amend the Constitution".

Article 46.4
A Bill containing a proposal or proposals for the amendment of this Constitution shall not contain any other proposal.

Article 46.5
A Bill containing a proposal for the amendment of this Constitution shall be signed by the President forthwith upon his being satisfied that the provisions of this Article have been complied with in respect thereof and that such proposal has been duly approved by the people in accordance with the provisions of section I of Article 47 of this Constitution and shall be duly promulgated by the President as a law.

Article 47.1
Every proposal for an amendment of this Constitution which is submitted by Referendum to the decision of the people shall, for the purpose of Article 46 of this Constitution, be held to have been approved by the people, if, upon having been so submitted, a majority of the votes cast at such Referendum shall have been cast in favour of its enactment into law.

Article 47.2.1°
Every proposal, other than a proposal to amend the Constitution, which is submitted by Referendum to the decision of the people shall be held to have been vetoed by the people if a majority of the votes cast at such Referendum shall have been cast against its enactment into law and if the votes so cast against its enactment into law shall have amounted to not less than thirty-three and one-third per cent. of the voters on the register.

Article 47.2.2°
Every proposal, other than a proposal to amend the Constitution, which is submitted by Referendum to the decision of the people shall for the purposes of Article 27 hereof be held to have been approved by the people unless vetoed by them in accordance with the provisions of the foregoing sub-section of this section.

Article 47.3
Every citizen who has the right to vote at an election for members of Dáil Éireann shall have the right to vote at a Referendum.

Article 47.4
Subject as aforesaid, the Referendum shall be regulated by law.

INDEX